a warm welcome

# a warm welcome

## HOW TO BE A GRACIOUS HOST TO FRIENDS AND FAMILY

### AMY ELLIOTT

RYLAND
PETERS
& SMALL
LONDON  NEW YORK

**Senior Designer** Toni Kay
**Commissioning Editor** Annabel Morgan
**Picture Research** Emily Westlake
**Production** Ros Holmes
**Art Director** Leslie Harrington
**Publishing Director** Alison Starling

First published in the
United Kingdom in 2009 by
Ryland Peters & Small
20–21 Jockey's Fields
London WC1R 4BW

First published in the United States
in 2009 by Ryland Peters & Small, Inc.
519 Broadway, 5th Floor
New York, NY 10012
www.rylandpeters.com

10 9 8 7 6 5 4 3 2 1

Text copyright © Fiona Beckett, Susannah
Blake, Linda Collister, Ross Dobson, Louise
Pickford, Ben Reed, Fran Warde and
Ryland Peters & Small 2009 Design and
all commissioned photography copyright
© Ryland Peters & Small 2009. For further
copyright information, see page 126.

Library of Congress Cataloging-in-
Publication Data

Elliott, Amy.
  Warm welcome : how to be a gracious
host to friends and family / Amy
Elliott.
    p. cm.
  ISBN 978-1-84597-851-8
1. Entertaining. 2. Cookery. I. Title.
TX731.E4176 2009
642'.4--dc22

                    2008050129

Printed in China

# Contents

# Introduction

Being a "good hostess" to overnight guests doesn't mean your approach to their accommodations, meals, and events has to be groundbreaking, or remarkably creative. In fact, hosting friends or family for several days at a time simply requires anticipating their basic needs, and fulfilling these needs with warmth and enthusiasm. Doing so with a certain amount of flair and ingenuity is great if you are so inclined. But I've found that a little forethought combined with lowkey-but-loving attention to detail will impress guests a great deal more than lavishly set tables, epic feasts, or elaborate plans and projects. That's where *A Warm Welcome* comes in. In it, I have simply outlined the essentials of hospitality—with a few modern provisions and details thrown in to keep things lighthearted and realistic.

Whatever your resources and time constraints, you have only to prepare your home to its fullest potential, pour drinks liberally, and do your best to ensure that everyone's having a good time. And remember that the reason your guests have come is to spend time with you, and to experience where and how you live, no matter the circumstances.

Full disclosure: I live in a one-bedroom apartment that spans 400 square feet/ 37 square meters. So this book presents a mix of what I practice and the kind of hostessing I aspire to. Once, anticipating a long-distance boyfriend's visit, I bought a new set of white-and-yellow sheets, imagining how they would look in my bedroom when sunlight poured through the windows. Like a gentlewoman preparing her residence for a king, I filled a vase with yellow lilies, and chilled a bottle of the best Champagne I could afford. When my mother stays, I bring her coffee in bed. And when I host friends from out of town, I suggest plans, draw maps, and happily comply with requests to attend the theater or to dine out at a glamorous restaurant.

And if I had the luxury of space? Well, then I would indeed make up the beds with ironed sheets. I would set a table for ten and tuck sprigs of fresh rosemary into the napkins. I would light a log fire and hand out steaming mugs of hot buttered rum. Then, I would thank my guests for coming, commit the moment to memory, and snap a photo to preserve it forever.

**Amy Elliott**
Brooklyn, New York

# PREPARATIONS

# *Preliminary considerations*

Entertaining several overnight houseguests is a more intimate experience than gathering a group around a dinner table for a few hours. So when you compose your guest list, carefully consider the resulting dynamic. College friends and coworkers may not mix; certain family members may be embroiled in a disagreement. Jane is vehement about her political views, John doesn't drink, this friend's a flirt, and that one's a drama queen… As the host, it's your responsibility to create the perfect balance of "life of the party" and "go with the flow" personalities.

Extend invitations via phone or email. Are the children invited, too? What about Nikita, their Siberian husky? Address these questions before they are asked. Mail paper invitations if the purpose of the getaway is to celebrate an event, such as an engagement party or a 40th birthday. Be sure to communicate the length of stay you have in mind—inviting someone to "stay the weekend" can translate to a variety of timeframes. It might mean "Friday evening through Sunday morning," or "late-afternoon Saturday till noon on Sunday." If you're flexible on your guests' exact arrival and departure times, so much the better, but do be clear about the number of days and nights.

## The week before

Furnish your guests with maps and detailed directions. Also let them know what they should bring (swimming attire, hiking shoes, club clothes for a night out on the town, a tuxedo for a black-tie New Year's Eve party, a sweater because it gets cold at night). Ask if there's anything special they'd like to eat or drink so that you can add these items to your shopping list, and find out if there's anything particular they would like to do while they're in town so that you can research the necessary arrangements and make reservations.

Finally—and you knew this was coming—give your house a thorough clean. In rooms that aren't used often, dust off all surfaces, including light bulbs, lampshades, ceiling fans, and paintwork. Arrange some fresh flowers to display in your sitting or dining room. Think through sleeping arrangements and check that you have enough bedding to accommodate everyone; use the majority of your time to spruce up every inch of the guest room.

# Preparing the guest room

Once you've tidied up the space, devote your attention to the small details that will make the experience of staying in your guest room all the more comfortable and inviting. So if your guest room is also your junk room or an office, restore it to its original glory: a beautifully styled, thoughtfully prepared retreat for your out-of-town visitors. For the time being, at least, find another home for your financial files, that ribbon-tied bundle of love letters from your college boyfriend, and the pile of holiday gifts you never got around to returning. If you use the chest of drawers as an extension of your personal wardrobe (are any extra buttons and other bits and bobs hiding in the top drawer?), remove your things so that your guest may fill the drawers with his or her own personal items. If there is a TV, make sure the remote control is in full working order and kept in a logical place.

When you show guests to their room, point out all the light switches and explain the particulars of opening and closing the drapes and window shades. Finally, some guests retain memories of overnight stays in an older relative's home, where the guest room was a stately, museum-like space—and there were harsh words for any child who dared to handle the curios or poke through the drawers. So make it abundantly clear to all guests that they are welcome, and in fact encouraged, to use anything and everything in the room as they please.

ON THE DRESSING TABLE
A tray for jewelry and watches
Fresh, long-lasting flowers
    arranged in a vase (skip this
    if there are allergy issues)
Hand mirror

ON THE NIGHTSTAND
Alarm clock
Box of tissues
Bottle of water and glasses
Reading light

IN THE CLOSET
Ample space for hanging garments
Extra pillows and blankets
Folding luggage stand
One-size-fits-all bathrobe
    and slippers
Selection of hangers (sturdy
    wooden ones for coats, padded
    satiny ones for delicate items,
    and the kind used for skirts)

STASHED IN A DRAWER
Eyeglass cleaner
Hand cream
Hot water bottle
Sewing kit

NEAR A WINDOW SEAT
OR READING CHAIR
Interesting books
Cozy throw
Daily newspaper
Up-to-date magazines

ON THE DESK
Computer, with its internet
    log-in instructions written
    neatly on a card
Phone
Letter opener and pens
Stamps / unisex stationery

# Time for bed

If you gloss over every other detail when preparing your home for guests, make sure you at least give your undivided attention to the making of the guest bed. Use the newest, nicest sheets in your linen closet and, if you have the luxury of time, wash them again, let them line-dry in the sun, then iron them to fancy-hotel perfection. Failing that, smooth all wrinkles on fitted and flat sheets with your hands (the flat sheet should be placed onto the bed with the hem at the top, print side down). Pull the bedspread taut, leaving enough fabric to drape over the pillows; if you're making the bed with a plush comforter or duvet, the pillows can rest on top of it, at the head of the bed. A pile of coordinating throw pillows makes a bed look more put-together, the way colorful accessories always punch up the chic factor of an outfit.

| ITEM | LAUNDERING FREQUENCY | SHELF LIFE |
| --- | --- | --- |
| BATH TOWELS | Once a week | About three to five years, or until you notice a decrease in absorbency, and/or a lingering mildew smell |
| SHEETS AND PILLOWCASES | Once a week | Ten years (earlier if they start to appear dingy) |
| QUILTS AND BLANKETS | Once a month | Five years |
| DOWN COMFORTER OR DUVET | Once or twice a year | Ten years |
| PILLOWS | Twice a year (more if you have allergies); throw them in the dryer with a few tennis balls to fluff them | Two to three years (ten percent of the weight of a two-year-old pillow can be attributed to dead mites and their droppings) |

### How to fluff a pillow

To make your guest bedroom pillows marshmallow-plump, hold each pillow horizontally and grasp the top two corners firmly. Shake vigorously to redistribute the filler evenly. Then, strike the front and back of the pillow, palm open, several times to further fluff the filler.

# The guest bath

You'll obviously want to clean the bathrooms your guests will be using, perhaps even more fastidiously than you normally would. Clean the soap dish and replenish the soap; leave out paper or linen guest towels. Check that drains, toilets, and locks are working properly and fix them if they're not. Also replace any light bulbs and take a moment to rid the medicine chest of any expired (or questionable) items.

Each guest should receive a set of towels to use during their stay; you can assign each guest a different color and leave a set of towels on his or her bed, stacked largest to smallest (knotting a ribbon around each stack would be an elegant touch but, of course, isn't necessary). Finally, see that the shower is stocked with the standard amenities (guests may or may not bring their own shampoo, conditioner, and soap) and place a beautifully wrapped, fresh bar of hand soap on or near the sink.

## ESSENTIALS

### BASIC AMENITIES
*Bar of soap*
*Bath gel, salts, or oil*
*Body lotion*
*Cotton balls*
*Disposable razors*
*Drinking cup*
*Extra rolls of toilet paper*
*Facecloth*
*Hand towels*
*Mouthwash*
*Shampoo and conditioner*
*Shower cap*
*Shower gel*
*Tissues*
*Toothpaste*
*Aspirin or ibuprofen*

### UPON REQUEST
*Allergy medicine*
*Aloe gel*
*Antacid*
*Antibiotic cream*
*Bandages*
*Extra toothbrush*
*Facial cleanser*
*Dental floss*
*Hairbrush and comb*
*Manicure kit*
*Nail polish remover*
*Stain remover*
*Sunscreen*

# Child- and animal-proofing your home

### CHILD'S PLAY

If your guests are traveling with children, special considerations need to be made in advance of their arrival. For example, babies start crawling at around 6–9 months, and their newfound mobility means accidents are always a possibility, especially in unfamiliar environments.

By the time babies start walking, the potential for mishaps increases; toddlers are unpredictable, fast-moving, and curious. If you're anxious about hosting a very young guest, know that you have the right to deem certain rooms of the house "off limits" and that making certain requests of parents (e.g. "Could you please keep Tommy out of the kitchen while I'm cooking?") is acceptable and may be necessary at times. While most parents keep close watch over their little ones, especially in someone else's home, there are ways to make a child-free situation a little more child-friendly:

- Invest in a few safety latches, baby gates for stairs, and power outlet covers if your guests are planning a long stay.
- Remove any small items that have fallen to the floor—coins, pebbles, and paperclips are a choking hazard.
- Any breakable knickknacks should be put out of reach or packed away. Ditto any toy-like collectibles that may be tempting to small children.

- If you have a pet, place his or her food and litter box in a child-free zone. Small, easily frightened animals, like birds, should be temporarily relocated to this area for the duration of the visit.
- Move cleaning supplies to higher cabinets or to the garage.
- Keep toilet lids closed.
- Keep beauty products, perfumes, razors, and medication out of reach.
- When cooking, use the stove's back burners. Turn the handles of pots and pans towards the back of the stove.
- Add knives to table settings after adults have been seated.

### ANIMAL INSTINCTS

If you don't have pets of your own, you understandably may be worried about a furry, four-legged creature running through your house, and interacting with your furniture, no matter how cute a dog or cat he or she is! The good news is that guests who arrive with Fido or Fluffy in tow will be so appreciative of your willingness to make such an accommodation that they'll be extra meticulous about policing their little darling's behavior. Meanwhile, here's what you can do to prepare your territory for invasion:

- Fragile items should be put away for the time being. A large dog's wagging tail can upend coffee-table curios; cats like high places and will find ways to jump up on high shelves and counters.
- Pills like aspirin and ibuprofen may be lethal if ingested by an animal. Don't leave them out.
- Common foods, such as chocolate, macadamia nuts, and onions, are harmful to animals.
- Some houseplants and flowers, including lilies, tulips, and irises, are also potentially dangerous. Temporarily place them somewhere out of sight or out of reach.
- Tuck exposed electrical cords out of the way.
- Let your guests know if you have recently fertilized your lawn or sprayed pesticides. Animals should be kept away from these areas for at least 24 hours.
- Remove ant or roach traps from areas a pet might be keen to explore.

# *If you are the guest...*

**Ask about attire** Do you need to bring a swimsuit? Are there any special parties or functions planned and, if so, what would be appropriate to wear? What will the weather be like when you're in town?

**Pack light**, especially if you are visiting someone who lives in a small apartment. It's terribly inconsiderate to traipse into someone else's home followed by a huge caravan of suitcases, sporting equipment, and a sack of your child's beach toys. Ignore this point if it's a holiday visit and you are merely bringing in presents, or if you have a little one and all that "baggage" is actually essential baby gear.

**Notify your host of any dietary restrictions**, food allergies, and quirks well in advance so that he or she can plan menus and shop for groceries accordingly. If you require certain creature comforts—carrot juice, for example, soy milk, or the only cereal your child will eat would all qualify—make these requests well in advance, or bring the items with you.

**If you are traveling by plane**, forward your itinerary to your host so that she can check the flight status. This is helpful and courteous even if your host is not picking you up at the airport; if she knows there's been a delay, she'll know she has a little extra time to load the dishwasher, throw in a load of laundry, or return a phone call.

**Establish an estimated arrival time** and stick to it. If you get a late start, miss your train, or run into traffic, call the host and let her know. Again, this information will free her to up to do an errand or maybe even grab a nap.

**Never bring a pet or a child without asking first** Pets are especially controversial—there may be allergies to consider, small children, a resident dog or cat who doesn't do well with other critters, brand-new carpeting...

**If you know your host** is entertaining several guests over the weekend, ask if you should bring your own towels and sheets.

# *Etiquette* Q & A

**Q** IS IT INCONSIDERATE OF ME TO INVITE MY SINGLE GIRLFRIEND TO STAY THE WEEKEND WITH A GROUP OF MARRIED COUPLES? I DON'T WANT HER TO FEEL UNCOMFORTABLE. AND WHILE I DO WORRY ABOUT HER THROWING OFF THE MALE/FEMALE RATIO, IT SEEMS RUDE NOT TO INVITE HER. I'M JUST NOT SURE HOW TO PROCEED HERE.

**A** When hosting a group, personalities are more important than marital status, and male/female ratios are less important than hurting someone's feelings. Always invite singletons to group gatherings, even if everyone else has a partner. Let the single guest herself decide if she's up for it and, of course, always make it clear that she may bring a date or a pal. It's great if you can invite another single person—male or female—to the gathering, to round things out. If you yourself don't know someone, ask your married guests to invite someone they know.

**Q** I'VE GOT ONE GUEST SLEEPING IN THE GUEST ROOM ON FRIDAY NIGHT ONLY, AND I'M EXPECTING ANOTHER GUEST TO COME AND STAY A FEW DAYS WITH ME STARTING ON SUNDAY. DO I HAVE TO CHANGE THE SHEETS IN BETWEEN THESE TWO VISITS? I'D RATHER NOT.

**A** Yes. Please. However, you're allowed a tiny bit of leeway if these two guests are related to each other. At the very least, change the pillowcases.

Q I LIVE IN A ONE-BEDROOM APARTMENT, WITH A PULL-
OUT COUCH IN THE LIVING ROOM. WHEN AM I OBLIGED
TO OFFER MY GUESTS MY BED AND SLEEP ON THE COUCH?

A Here are the circumstances that would call for you to give up your bed:
a) You are hosting a guest who is older than you; b) You are hosting a guest who
is pregnant; c) You are hosting a guest who has back problems. You can make
a sofa mattress more comfortable by investing in a feather pad to place on top
of it (failing that, use an old down comforter or duvet).

Q UH-OH... WE INVITED A COUPLE AND FORGOT TO MAKE IT CLEAR
THAT WE WANT THE WEEKEND TO BE ADULTS-ONLY. WE DON'T HAVE
CHILDREN, AND NEITHER DO OUR NEIGHBORS (WHOM WE'LL BE
SPENDING TIME WITH), AND I KNOW THAT THE PRESENCE OF A FOUR-
AND FIVE-YEAR-OLD IS GOING TO ALTER THE MOOD OF THE WEEKEND.
HOW DO WE TELL OUR FRIENDS THAT THEIR KIDS HAVE TO STAY HOME?

A Guests should never assume that their children are invited unless the host has said so
explicitly. Still, close friends and relatives are likely to forget or ignore this point, which is why it's
very important to communicate that the weekend is adults-only when you first extend the invitation.
If you haven't done so, simply call your friends and say, "I'm so sorry, I forgot to mention that we're
trying to keep this visit adults-only. Do you think you'll be able to leave Sally and Ellie with your in-
laws?" If getting a babysitter isn't possible for the weekend in question, be willing to switch the
date... or to have the kids come after all.

ARRIVALS

WELCOME!
*Benvenuto (Italian)*
*Bienvenidos (Spanish)*
*Bienvenue (French)*
*Huan ying (Mandarin)*
*Willkommen (German)*
*Yokoso (Japanese)*
*Welkom (Dutch)*
*Välkommen (Swedish)*
*Kalos orisate (Greek)*
*Swaagatam (Hindi)*
*Bem-vindo (Portuguese)*
*Dobro pozhalovat (Russian)*
*Hwangyong-hamnida (Korean)*
*Witamy (Polish)*

ESSENTIALS

# *Welcome!*

If you're an enthusiastic, effervescent person, the instinct to greet your guests with a cheerful salutation and a spontaneous embrace comes naturally. If you tend to be more reserved, or are perhaps feeling somewhat stressed about preparing dinner or the prospect of the visit in general, do your best to extend a warm welcome. Guests don't want to walk into a home and feel as if their presence is intrusive or agitating.

Ideally, the minute a guest enters your home, your spouse or an able child would take her bags to her room, allowing you to get down to the business of offering refreshments. Often the request will be for water; soon after, a glass of wine or a cocktail will surely be in order (see pages 46–55 for ideas).

Some guests like to flop down on a chair and get the party started immediately, while others may want to retire to their rooms to unpack, freshen up, and change their clothes. At some point, you should give guests a quick tour of your home, pointing out light switches, locks, any tricky faucets, and the multitude of miscellaneous details that make your home unique.

Keep dinner low-key—weary travelers may not fully appreciate the grandeur of a fancy feast. And while it may be tempting to spend that first night drinking and chatting till all hours of the night, it's best to retire early and save your energy for the rest of the visit.

LEAVE THE LIGHT ON... ILLUMINATED PORCH LIGHTS ENABLE YOUR GUESTS TO SPOT YOUR HOUSE NUMBER (IF THEY'RE DRIVING), AND LETS THEM KNOW THAT YOU'RE LOOKING FORWARD TO THEIR ARRIVAL.

# Granola

*This crunchy granola is delicious for breakfast or even just as a tasty nibble straight from the jar. The more maple syrup you add, the crunchier the mixture will be.*

2¼ cups / 300 g old-fashioned rolled oats

⅔ cups / 100 g almonds, chopped

2 tablespoons / 30 g pumpkin seeds

2 tablespoons / 30 g sunflower seeds

1 tablespoon / 15 g sesame seeds

1 cup / 250 ml pure maple syrup

¼ cup / 100 g dried apricots

¼ cup / 100 g sultanas

2 tablespoons / 20 g nonfat dry / powdered milk

**SERVES 4**

Preheat the oven to 325°F (170°C) Gas 3 and line a baking sheet with parchment.

Put the oats, almonds, and seeds in a bowl and mix well. Spread on the baking sheet in an even layer and drizzle with the maple syrup. Put in the oven and bake for 25 minutes.

Remove the baking sheet, add the dried fruit and dry milk, and mix well. Return to the oven and bake for a further 15 minutes, until the mixture is crisp and golden.

Let cool, then store in an airtight container.

# *Bright and early*

### RED-EYE OPENER

Offering guests some sort of refreshment upon arrival is one of the cornerstones of entertaining etiquette.

Guests who arrive very early in the morning may well decline and opt to retire to bed immediately, but others will no doubt be eager to sit down to a restorative, invigorating mini breakfast. Don't overload a bleary-eyed traveler with heavy food that's hard to digest; instead, keep it light and refreshing with fresh fruit, mild cheeses, or a bowl of granola and yogurt and a glass of fresh juice.

## *St Clement's punch*

*This is a fresh, zesty, citrus-based punch that's packed with vitamin C.*

1 cup/250 ml freshly squeezed orange juice (about 4 oranges)
⅔ cup/150 ml freshly squeezed pink grapefruit juice (1–2 grapefruit)
1 cup/250 ml traditional cloudy lemonade, chilled

slices of orange and lemon, to garnish

**SERVES 4–6**

Pour the orange and grapefruit juices into a jug, top up with the lemonade, and stir well. Add a few slices of orange and lemon to the jug and serve. If you're feeling indulgent, add a tablespoon of Grand Marnier for a little extra edge!

### IT'S CUSTOMARY

*In Japan, you must remove shoes before entering the home. Your host will provide slippers to wear inside.*

*In Russia, it is considered rude to turn down shots of vodka or other alcoholic refreshment.*

*In Brazil, men greet each other by shaking hands, while women kiss on both cheeks.*

*In Switzerland, the "three-kiss" rule applies: You kiss the right cheek, the left cheek, and end with a third kiss on the right cheek.*

*In France, guests should not bring a bottle of wine as a gift (it implies that the hosts do not have good taste).*

*In Egypt, guests do not bring their hosts flowers as a gift. Chocolates or pastries are preferred.*

# After dark

### LATE ARRIVALS

Guests who arrive late at night are almost certain to be hungry—serve something small, but comforting, to make them feel sleepy and to ready them, ultimately, for a nice long rest. A sandwich, slice of cake, or piece of pie with a glass of milk would be ideal, as would a cup of tomato soup with some cheese and crackers. Rich, spicy foods may interfere with your visitor's ability to get to sleep, and many chocolate desserts have a stimulating effect that might also make it difficult to unwind. A glass of wine or a hot, boozy drink might be the best way to help soothe and relax a guest who needs to decompress before climbing into bed.

### MINI MIDNIGHT REPAST

Bagels are usually considered a brunch item, but they have the benefit of being easy to put together at short notice and also offer a substantial snack. The classic smoked salmon and cream cheese filling adds a touch of elegance. And if your guests aren't hungry, you can serve the bagels for breakfast instead!

## Toasted bagels with cream cheese and smoked salmon

*Toasted bagels are the ideal snack for a tired, travelworn new arrival.*

2 bagels
½ cup/100 g cream cheese
4 oz./125 g sliced smoked salmon
lemon wedges, for squeezing
freshly ground black pepper

**SERVES 2**

Split the bagels in half horizontally and toast on both sides in a toaster, under the broiler/grill, or using a stove-top grill pan.

Spread the bottom half of each bagel with a layer of cream cheese and fold the slices of smoked salmon on top. Squeeze over plenty of lemon juice, sprinkle with freshly ground black pepper, and serve immediately, topped with the second half of the bagel.

# If you are the guest...

**Bring a gift** to show your appreciation! It's not a mandatory gesture, but so many people choose to observe this tradition that you run the risk of appearing impolite if you don't follow suit.

**Your gift needn't be expensive** and can be as simple as flowers from your garden or a selection of pastries to enjoy at breakfast the next morning. If you know your host well, you can pick up items with her interests and/or décor in mind, or choose something she would be unlikely to buy for herself (luxurious hand soaps, for example) but is certain to enjoy. In addition, it's nice to bring storybooks for small children, and a special toy for the family pet.

**It's certainly very charming** to show your gratitude during your stay versus presenting a gift on arrival. Many guests like to pick up their host a little trinket when they're out and about, and take their cues from conversations held during their stay. If your host raves about a wine she sampled recently, or mentions a book she's longing to read, you'll know just the thing to get her, and she's sure to be tickled pink by your clever detective work. But the classic (and undeniably classy) gesture is to arrive on the doorstep with a "hostess gift" in hand.

GREAT GIFT IDEAS

*A homemade pie*

*An obscure, exotic liqueur*

*Artisanal olive oil*

*Birdhouse*

*Bookends*

*Cake stand*

*Candles*

*Candlesticks*

*Caviar*

*Cheeseboard and knife*

*Christmas tree ornaments*

*Coasters*

*Cookie jar*

*Drawer sachets*

*Fancy chocolates*

*Festive table runner*

*Fresh, seasonal, farm-stand fruit*

*Gourmet tea, coffee, or cocoa*

*Homemade cookies or candy*

*Honey*

*Monogrammed stationery*

*Napkin rings*

*Photo album*

*Picnic basket*

*Place cards*

*Quirky vintage etiquette or
    decorating books*

*Room fragrance*

*Salt shaker and pepper mill*

*Scented linen water or spray*

*Table-ready plant or floral
    arrangement*

*Vintage apron*

*Watering can*

*Windchime*

*Wine*

# *Etiquette* Q & A

Q I'M WORRIED ABOUT SHOWER LOGISTICS. I'VE GOT ONE BATHROOM AND THIS WEEK I AM HOSTING A CROWD OF EIGHT! HOW DO I ACCOMMODATE EVERYONE'S NEEDS IN AN UNOBTRUSIVE WAY THAT DOESN'T SEEM LIKE I'M MICROMANAGING THEIR BATHING HABITS?

A Even the most abundant hot water supply is unlikely to withstand eight back-to-back showers in the morning, so it's sensible to discuss shower schedules before retiring to bed the night before. Some guests may be puzzled by your giving this matter any thought at all, but they'll soon understand if they find themselves taking an ice-cold shower. When you bring the hot water issue to your guests' attention, you can suggest that they stagger shower times, perhaps with some guests showering in the morning and others in the afternoon. Lots of hosts jump into the shower the moment they get up, before preparing breakfast, to free up the bathroom for their guests. Another good reason to stagger showers is that waiting for everyone to get ready, one after the other, can delay the start of daytime activities significantly, which would be a shame if you have planned a special outing.

The topic of shower schedules also bears mentioning if someone, perhaps yourself, has to be up and ready to go at a certain time. For example, if you're working one day, and usually take a shower at 7:30 a.m., it's a good idea to let your guests know so that they can plan to shower either before or after you.

**Q** Is it okay to politely ask guests to refrain from smoking in our home? What if the guest happens to be my father-in-law?

**A** No guest should ever light up in your home without asking, and this most certainly also applies to family members. Most smokers are used to being banished to front doorsteps and back porches when they want a cigarette anyway, and your father-in-law should be no exception. If he objects, your husband should be the one to explain/enforce the house rule. If there are children around, your father-in-law may be more inclined to comply with your request, as smoking in front of little ones is a widely acknowledged faux pas, thanks to the known dangers of secondhand smoke (and because adults who smoke set a bad example).

**Q** My guest's flight arrives at 3 a.m. Am I expected to pick her up at the airport? If she takes a taxi, she'll get to my house around 4 a.m. After I get up and let her in, can I return to bed?

**A** Three a.m? Absolutely not! Airport pickups are never mandatory, but are appreciated if you can manage it time- and distance-wise, especially if you're hosting family members, or someone very young or very old. Otherwise, guests can be trusted to handle their own transportation arrangements. They should do everything possible to arrive at a reasonable hour, but sometimes this can't be avoided.

If a guest is scheduled to arrive at your home in the wee hours of the morning, you must of course welcome her warmly, offer her refreshment, and show her to her room, but don't feel obliged to roll out the red carpet. Once you have seen to her immediate needs, you are well within your rights to return to bed. A polite way to flee the scene: "If it's all right with you, I'm going to try to get a little more sleep. Make yourself at home and I'll see you in a few hours."

# MEALS AND MERRIMENT

# Feeding friends

Enjoying meals together is often the highlight of a visit, both for the guests and their host. The only problem, no matter how skilled a chef you are, is that orchestrating fancy, complicated meals robs you of valuable time with your visitors. (Of course, if you are trying to avoid certain guests, busying yourself in the kitchen is a great way to dodge them without appearing rude!)

So now's the time to trot out your most reliable recipes and devise the kind of daily menus you'll be able to execute quickly and confidently. To help you decide upon the final menus, be realistic about the amount of effort the meals will require, as well as what you can afford to spend on the ingredients. Also, take your guests' tastes into account; a gourmet extravaganza may be lost on the very young or very conservative, while religious or vegetarian diet restrictions (not to mention the occasional disagreeable tummy) may mean certain foods are out of the question.

In general, seasonal, festive but simply prepared fare such as grilled meats, hearty soups and stews, vegetables from your garden, and homemade pies and cakes will always be well received. Shop for groceries accordingly, taking numbers of guests into account, as well as any food-related habits and/or passions. If Aunt Louise prefers sweetener in her coffee instead of sugar, add this item to your list; if your college roommate's husband is mad for jellybeans, imagine how thrilled he'll be when he discovers you've bought some just for him.

# Breakfast time

You're entitled to lots of flexibility when it comes to navigating the beginning of the day. The host may sleep as late as she likes just as long as she has let her guests know she may do so, and has seen to their morning needs in advance.

For example, early risers need to know what the coffee- or tea-making situation is (leave out written instructions if necessary, so that they may tend to this detail themselves). If you often sleep late, tell guests explicitly that they may help themselves to whatever they like in the kitchen and pantry. Let them know the night before if you're planning to make pancakes or omelets for a sit-down breakfast so that they don't take matters into their own hands. (If you have agreed to make breakfast, plan to get up no later than 9:30 a.m.)

If a guest asks to be woken at a certain time (for a flight, or a meeting, let's say), either hand him an alarm clock, or wake him yourself by knocking lightly on the bedroom door and saying "Good morning, it's 6:30" in a whisper. When the wake-up time is this early, you are well within your rights to return to bed (but if you have the energy, why not prepare his breakfast beverage of choice and offer a bagel or muffin?)

Finally, you may be a "morning person" and your guests may loathe this time of day. Be sensitive to people's individual rhythms and preference for quiet conversation, not effervescent chatter. Wait till they've properly woken up and regained their usual disposition before discussing the day's events or proposing plans.

## Simple scrambled eggs

*To make more, a good rule of thumb is two eggs per person and one tablespoon of milk per egg.*

1 tablespoon butter
4 eggs
4 tablespoons milk (not nonfat)
sea salt and freshly ground black pepper
snipped chives, to garnish (optional)

**SERVES 2**

Melt the butter in a nonstick skillet/frying pan over a medium–low heat. Meanwhile, in a mixing bowl, combine the eggs and milk with a dash of salt and pepper. Beat the egg mixture with a whisk until well blended.

After the butter has melted completely, pour the egg mixture into the pan. As the eggs begin to set, use a wooden spoon to scrape the sides of the pan and fold the eggs over themselves. When no liquid remains and the eggs are moist, but not runny, spoon onto buttered toast and sprinkle with a few chives, if using. Serve immediately.

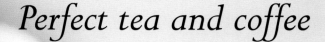

# Perfect tea and coffee

If you are among the select few who do not rely on a caffeinated beverage to start the day, never agree to host overnight guests unless you're prepared to offer them coffee and tea (most people prefer one or the other) in the morning.

## THE PERFECT CUP OF COFFEE

Passionate coffee drinkers are particular about their brewing methods (and almost none will involve an automatic drip coffeemaker). If you're hosting a coffee fanatic, you don't have to meet their high standards to the letter (or invest in any fancy equipment, or pay a small fortune for coffee beans…) but do consider upgrading and perfecting your coffee-making technique (or lack thereof).

Filtered water and freshly ground beans (your vendor can do this for you at no extra charge; the type of coffeemaker and filter you use will dictate how coarse or fine the coffee should be) make a huge difference. As for the proper coffee/water ratio, two level tablespoons of coffee per 6 oz./180 ml cup of water is the golden rule, but feel free to experiment. Arriving at the ratio that yields the best-tasting results will depend on your equipment and preferred type of bean, roast, or blend. If you find that you prefer a brew that's less robust, keep in mind that coffee junkies would generally much prefer a cup that's too strong rather than too weak, so measure liberally when you're entertaining them— and dilute your cup of Joe with milk.

## A PROPER CUP OF TEA

A "proper" cup of tea is also a matter of personal taste. For best results, follow this very basic formula: Use one teaspoon of loose-leaf tea or one tea bag for every cup of tea you wish to make and steep for three minutes (for a tea bag) and up to five minutes (for loose-leaf tea), depending on how strong your guest likes it.

Use filtered water and allow it to boil only if you're making black or herbal tea (to avoid ruining their subtle, delicate flavor, white and green teas should be steeped with water well below boiling point). If you are steeping tea in a teapot, make sure you "scald" it first—warm the pot by pouring in some hot water, or some water from the kettle before it begins to boil, then discard it before brewing. This step will help keep your brewed tea nice and hot for a longer period of time.

# Lemon, almond, and blueberry muffins

*Everyone loves a blueberry muffin, and these are extra-special, packed with ground almonds. Whip up a batch and leave them in a tin beside your tea and coffee supplies, so guests can help themselves in the morning.*

⅓ cup/50 g whole blanched almonds

1¾ cups/250 g all-purpose/plain flour, sifted

1 tablespoon baking powder, sifted

⅓ cup/85 g golden caster sugar

grated zest of 1 unwaxed lemon

1 large egg

1¼ cups/280 ml milk

2 teaspoons freshly squeezed lemon juice

¼ cup/4 tablespoons vegetable oil

1 cup/150 g fresh or frozen blueberries (use straight from the freezer)

*a deep 12-hole muffin tin, well greased*

**MAKES 12 MUFFINS**

Put the almonds in a food processor or blender and grind to a coarse meal. They should have more texture than commercially ground almonds. Transfer to a large bowl and mix with the flour, baking powder, sugar, and lemon zest.

Lightly beat the egg with the milk, lemon juice, and vegetable oil. Add to the dry ingredients and stir just enough to make a coarse, lumpy mixture. Add the blueberries and mix quickly, using as few strokes as possible, leaving the mixture slightly streaky.

Do not beat or overmix, or the muffins will be tough and dry.

Spoon the mixture into the prepared muffin tin, filling each hole about two-thirds full. Bake in a preheated oven at 400°F (200°C) Gas 6 for about 20–25 minutes, until golden and firm to the touch.

Let the muffins cool in the tin for 1 minute, then turn out onto a wire rack. Eat warm, immediately, or within 24 hours. When thoroughly cooled, the muffins can be wrapped and frozen for up to 1 month.

# Brunch

Think of brunch as either a big, elaborate breakfast, or a light luncheon with a breakfasty bent; no matter how you interpret it, this meal is traditionally served after breakfast time and before afternoon tea. That timeframe might constitute any period between the hours of 11 a.m. and 4 p.m.

Brunch is an ideal meal to prepare on a lazy Sunday, especially if you and your guests were up late the night before. You'll want to serve a mix of light and hearty, sweet and savory fare—a bowl of fruit salad, a frittata or quiche, a basket of freshly baked muffins, scones, or rolls, and poached salmon or a glistening baked ham would be delightful. And don't forget cocktails. Cheerful Bellinis (see page 51) or spicy Bloody Marys (see page 52), garnished with a ruffly stalk of celery, are colorful brunch classics.

(see page 51) or spicy Bloody Marys (see page 52)

**ESSENTIALS**

IF ANYONE'S HUNGOVER...
*It's easy to accidentally overindulge when you're having a good time. If you feel a little hungover one morning, chances are, your guests will share your pain. And if you feel fine—but know that some of your party stayed up "chatting" long after you called it a night—as the host, it's your responsibility to help your guests feel better fast.*

*Drinking excessively causes dehydration, so make sure everyone downs plenty of fluids. Have a pitcher of ice water and glasses on the kitchen table, along with a selection of vitamin-packed juices. If you have the energy, prepare a batch of banana milkshakes sweetened with honey (to soothe the stomach and replenish potassium, magnesium, and electrolytes).*

*The best food you can offer is something like a spinach and cheese omelet—avoid greasy, salty foods like bacon or French fries, which will further dehydrate the body. Technically, coffee can also have a dehydrating effect, but put a pot on anyway, as not offering what many consider a morning necessity might result in tears (or fisticuffs).*

## THE WELL-STOCKED BAR

*You can either follow these guidelines to the letter, or tailor them to the amount of space in your drinks cabinet / refrigerator, and the types of drinkers that you're entertaining.*

### Wines and spirits
*Bourbon, gin, red wine, rum, scotch, tequila, triple sec, vermouth (dry and sweet), vodka, whiskey, white wine.*

### Mixers
*Club soda / soda water, cola, cranberry juice, ginger ale, orange juice, Rose's lime juice / cordial, tonic water.*

### Accessories
*Bottle opener, corkscrew, sharp knife, ice bucket / tongs, jigger, muddler, shaker, stirrer, strainer.*

### Garnishes
*Lemons, limes, maraschino cherries, olives, onions, tabasco.*

### Optional (but highly recommended)
*Angostura bitters, Champagne or sparkling wine, grenadine, horseradish, liqueurs (at least one—most people like Grand Marnier), port, top-shelf cognac or brandy, vin santo.*

# Welcoming drinks

There are many reasons to offer your guests a drink: to help them unwind after a long journey; to facilitate conversation among the members of a group who don't know each other very well; to enhance conversations among guests who are well acquainted; to inject an air of festivity into any given situation; or to kick off an action-packed night on the town. And don't forget there needn't be a reason at all… except, perhaps, the fact that it's six o'clock (or well after midnight, and no one wants to go to bed). On the following pages, you'll find recipes for all manner of drinks.

## A LEMON LESSON

**Wheels**  Cut off both tips of the lemon. Gently slit lengthwise, and then thinly slice, crosswise, into ¼ in/5 mm wheels. Each wheel will have its own little slit; place it on the glass so that it straddles the rim.

**Wedges**  Cut the lemon in half lengthwise. Next, place each lemon half pulp-side down on the cutting board. Now carefully slice each half crosswise to create ½ in/1.5 cm wedges.

**Twists**  Cut off both ends of the lemon. Insert a sharp knife (or use a spoon) to separate the lemon pulp from the rind. Cut the rind into ¼ in/5 mm strips. To create pretty curly shapes, use a lemon zester or a paring knife to cut a spiral into the lemon peel, from top to bottom. Cut the spiral into small pieces and reinforce the curl using a straw (or your finger).

# Cocktail classics

Every hostess must have a handle on the fundamentals of cocktail-making, and be able to expertly prepare and pour a gin and tonic, vodka and cranberry juice, scotch on the rocks, or a whiskey and soda.

Beyond these basics, the most sophisticated hosts are also familiar with other, more complicated, concoctions that have been considered cocktail "classics" for decades. Most of the following will require a cocktail shaker and a nice variety of glasses.

## Martini

*Nothing beats a good martini.*

a dash of vermouth (Noilly Prat or
Martini Extra Dry)
3 oz./75 ml well-chilled gin or vodka
an olive or lemon twist, to garnish

Add the ingredients to a mixing glass filled with ice and stir. Strain into a chilled martini glass and garnish with an olive or lemon twist.

## Gin & tonic

*Buy good tonic water in small
bottles, so you always have a fresh
one on hand. Flat tonic is a no-no!*

3 oz./75 ml well-chilled gin
tonic water, to top up
a lemon wedge

Pour the gin into a tumbler over ice. Top with the tonic water, garnish with the lemon wedge, and serve.

## Sidecar

*A classic drink created in the
1920s by Harry McElhone,
who founded Harry's New York
Bar in Paris.*

2 oz./50 ml brandy
1 oz./25 ml freshly squeezed
lemon juice
1 oz./25 ml Cointreau
sugar, for the glass

Shake all the ingredients together over ice and strain into a chilled martini glass with a sugared edge.

## Kir royale

*A touch of fizz and
sophistication!*

1 dash crème de cassis
Champagne, to top up

Add a small dash of crème de cassis to a champagne flute and gently top up with Champagne. Stir gently and serve.

## Margarita

*The classic tequila-based cocktail.*

2 oz./50 ml gold tequila
1 oz./25 ml triple sec or Cointreau
1 oz./25 ml freshly squeezed lime juice
salt, for the glass

Shake all the ingredients sharply with cracked ice, then strain into a chilled margarita glass edged with salt.

## Cuba libre

*This is essentially a rum and coke,
but with a generous twist of lime.*

3 lime wedges
2 oz./50 ml Cuban white rum
cola, to top up

Muddle the lime in a highball glass, fill with ice and add the rum and the cola. Stir gently and serve with two straws.

## Gimlet

*A zesty evening starter drink.*

2 oz./50 ml gin or vodka
1 oz./25 ml Rose's lime juice/cordial

Add the spirit and cordial/juice to a shaker filled with ice. Shake very sharply and double-strain into a chilled martini glass.

# Manhattan

*The perfect balance of sweet and dry; your guests will welcome this old-school favorite.*

2oz./50 ml rye whiskey
2 barspoons/12.5 ml sweet vermouth
2 barspoons/12.5 ml dry vermouth
2 dashes Angostura bitters
cocktail cherry, to garnish

Add the ingredients to a mixing glass filled with ice (they should already be very cold) and stir the mixture until chilled. Strain into a chilled cocktail glass, add the garnish, and serve.

# Fun and flirty

Girls-only gatherings call for drinks that are unabashedly sweet and indulgent. Champagne is a frequent ingredient—effervescent cocktails have a glamorous edge and, just as important, are guaranteed to inspire lively conversation. Whether you offer beverages that are sexy, sophisticated, or downright campy, there's something truly fun and festive about enjoying the kinds of drinks you might order in a tony nightclub within the privacy of your living room.

## Brandy Alexander

*This luscious, indulgent after-dinner cocktail is perfect for chocolate lovers.*

2 oz./50 ml brandy
1 oz./25 ml dark crème de cacao
1 oz./25 ml heavy/double cream
grated nutmeg, to garnish

Shake all the ingredients over ice and strain into a chilled martini glass. Garnish with a sprinkling of grated nutmeg.

## French 75

*A bubbly, tart cocktail devised during the First World War by American army officers.*

1 oz./25 ml gin
2 barspoons/12.5 ml freshly squeezed lemon juice
1 barspoon simple/sugar syrup
Champagne, to top up
lemon twist, to garnish

Shake the gin, lemon juice, and syrup over ice and strain into a Champagne flute. Top with Champagne and garnish with a lemon twist (see page 46).

## Bellini

*There's one golden rule for the perfect Bellini—always use ripe, fresh peaches to make the peach juice.*

½ fresh peach, blanched
2 barspoons/12.5 ml crème de pêche
1 dash peach bitters (optional)
Champagne, to top up
a peach ball, to garnish

Purée the peach in a blender and add to a champagne flute. Pour in the crème de pêche and the peach bitters, if using, and gently top up with champagne, stirring carefully and continuously. Garnish with a peach ball in the bottom of the glass, then serve.

## Flirtini

*Great for big groups, this martini is light, creamy, and simple to make in bulk.*

2 oz./50 ml vodka
1 large dash Chambord or crème de mure
3 oz./75 ml fresh pineapple juice

Add all the ingredients to a shaker filled with ice, shake sharply, and strain into a chilled martini glass.

## Cosmopolitan

*The ultimate Sex and the City girly drink.*

1¼ oz./35 ml lemon vodka
1 oz./25 ml triple sec
1 oz./25 ml freshly squeezed lime juice
1 oz./25 ml cranberry juice

Add all the ingredients to a shaker filled with ice, shake sharply, and strain into a chilled martini glass.

# Poolside

Get ready to break out your blender! Find a kitschy glass or melamine pitcher, if you've got one, for serving up these colorful drinks with a tropical, refreshing feel. You'll want to have plenty of ice on hand (crushed, for whipping up frothy favorites, and cubed for keeping juice-based drinks cool). When you're outside, disposable cups are better than glass ones because they won't shatter, but they're bad for the environment. Invest in some plastic goblets, highballs, and other barware to use instead. And have fun with garnishes!

## Pimm's

*Surprise your guests with this classic English summer sundowner.*

2 oz./50 ml Pimm's No. 1
4 oz./100 ml lemonade
2 oz./50 ml ginger beer
a cucumber slice
a lemon slice
an orange slice
a fresh strawberry
a mint sprig

Build all the ingredients in a highball glass filled with ice. Stir gently and serve with two straws.

## Daiquiri

*The perfect balance of golden rum, sharp citrus juice, and sweet sugar syrup.*

2 oz./50 ml golden rum
1 oz./25 ml freshly squeezed lime juice
2 barspoons simple/sugar syrup

Pour all the ingredients into an ice-filled shaker. Shake and strain into a chilled martini glass.

## Mai tai

*A rum-based cocktail with a tropical flair.*

2 oz./50 ml aged Jamaican rum
1 oz./25 ml freshly squeezed lime juice
1 oz./25 ml orgeat syrup
1 oz./25 ml orange curaçao
⅓ oz./10 ml simple/sugar syrup
a mint sprig, to garnish

Pour all the ingredients into an ice-filled shaker. Shake sharply, and strain into a rocks glass filled with ice. Garnish with a mint sprig.

## Bloody Mary

*The perfect spicy pick-me-up.*

2 oz./50 ml vodka
6 oz./150 ml tomato juice
⅔ oz./15 ml freshly squeezed lemon juice
4 dashes Worcestershire sauce
4 dashes Tabasco sauce
1 barspoon/6 ml creamed horseradish
a grind of black pepper
a grind of sea salt
a celery stick, to garnish

Add all the ingredients to a highball glass filled with ice. Stir well, garnish with a celery stick, and serve with two straws.

## Piña colada

*The ultimate poolside indulgence!*

2 oz./50 ml white rum
1¼ oz./35 ml coconut cream
2 oz./50 ml fresh pineapple juice
a pineapple spear, to garnish

Blend all the ingredients with a scoop of crushed ice and pour into a hurricane glass. Garnish with a pineapple spear.

# Mojito

*A refreshingly minty drink,
perfect for a hot day.*

2 lime wedges
2 barspoons/12.5 ml sugar
8 mint sprigs, plus one to garnish
2 oz./50 ml club soda/soda water
1 dash club soda/soda water
sugar/simple syrup, to taste

Muddle the lime, sugar,
and mint in the bottom of a
highball glass, fill with plenty
of crushed ice, and add the
rum. Stir well and add a dash
of club soda/soda water. Add
a dash or two of syrup, to
taste. Garnish with a mint
sprig and serve.

# Hot toddy

*A great winter warmer, and also*
*perfect for a thermos flask, if you plan*
*to take your guests for a brisk walk!*

5 whole cloves
2 lemon slices
2 oz./50 ml whiskey
1 oz./25 ml freshly squeezed
lemon juice
2 barspoons/12.5 ml honey
or simple/sugar syrup
3 oz./75 ml hot water
a cinnamon stick

Skewer the cloves into the lemon
slices and add them to a heatproof
glass along with the rest of the
ingredients. Stir well.

# Fireside

Most of us are used to sipping drinks that are cold, so serving winter warmers in steaming glass mugs has a certain novelty. It also has an "après ski" allure, sure to result in rosy cheeks, twinkling eyes, and snuggling beneath cozy blankets and throws. Accordingly, serve these drinks on very cold days, perhaps after outdoor activities, or as a way to mellow out after dinner and dessert.

## Blue blazer

*A fiery drink (literally!) that will wow your guests, but be warned—you may want to rehearse this before trying it in front of an audience.*

a sugar cube
4 oz./100 ml boiling water
4 oz./100 ml whiskey
grated nutmeg, to garnish

Warm two small metal tankards. In one, dissolve the sugar in the boiling water. Pour the whiskey into the other. Set the whiskey alight and, as it burns, pour the liquid into the first tankard and back, from one to the other, creating a continuous stream of fire. Once the flame has died down, pour the mixture into a warmed old-fashioned glass and garnish with grated nutmeg.

## Irish coffee

*A smooth, creamy treat for weary travelers.*

1¼ oz./35 ml Irish whiskey
a double espresso
⅓ oz./10 ml simple/sugar syrup
1 oz./25 ml heavy/double cream
3 coffee beans, to garnish

Mix the whiskey, espresso, and syrup in a heatproof glass, making sure the coffee is piping hot. Gently layer the cream over the surface of the coffee, using a flat-bottomed barspoon. Garnish with the coffee beans.

## Hot buttered rum

*The addition of butter gives this mulled rum drink extra richness.*

1 oz./25 ml dark rum
4 cloves
2 unwaxed lemon slices
2 teaspoons raw/unrefined sugar
10 oz./250ml just-boiled water
2 tablespoons/25 g unsalted butter
2 cinnamon sticks

Put the rum into two heatproof glasses and add the cloves, lemon slices and sugar. Top up with boiling water and add the butter. Put a cinnamon stick in each glass and stir the butter as it melts. Serve immediately.

## Mulled wine

*A beautiful spicy drink that will warm your friends' hearts.*

2 bottles red wine,
3 cups/750 ml each
8 whole cloves
2 oranges
3 tablespoons brown sugar
2 in/5 cm fresh ginger, peeled and chopped
1 cinnamon stick
½ teaspoon freshly grated nutmeg

**MAKES 12 GLASSES**

Pour the red wine into a saucepan. Insert the cloves in the oranges, then cut each orange into quarters. Add to the pan, together with the sugar, ginger, cinnamon, and nutmeg.

Heat the mixture to simmering point and simmer for 8–10 minutes, then serve hot.

# Snack time

The logical time to serve snacks is during cocktail hour, but you may find that children, and many adults, crave a snack in the late afternoon. People tend to return from the beach famished, for example, and if you plan to dine late, your guests may prefer to eat something snacky at tea-time, lest they fill up on too many cocktail-hour hors d'oeuvres before dinner.

Never put a guest in the awkward position of having to ask for food. In the kitchen, set out a generous bowl of nuts or dried apricots; a platter of crackers and peanut butter; and a plate of cookies for guests to nibble on at any time. Otherwise, let your guests know that they are welcome to help themselves to the contents of your pantry and fridge when they're feeling peckish.

# Lunchtime strategies

If you have young children yourself and more staying with you, it's a good idea to plan a simple lunch for them (you and the other parents can discuss what makes the most sense to prepare). But few adults will require a substantial sit-down lunch, especially if you've served a big breakfast. Have some light, easy-to-prepare fare on hand, such as good leftover soup or a loaf of fresh bread and sandwich provisions, but don't overload your guests with food. If they're not feeling hungry and you set out food for them, they may feel obliged to eat it, a move that could hamper their enjoyment of that evening's dinner (the hostess's tour de force). So do make it clear that you're happy to fix a little lunch for them, but that the meal itself is entirely optional.

On the other hand, afternoon outings may take you into town or out in the country, where a midday mealtime pitstop can add to the fun. You may decide to eat out at lunchtime, or you may have planned to embark on a picnic or to attend a neighbor's daytime barbecue. If this is the case, plan a light supper—a nice salad with assorted bruschetta, for example, and lemon sorbet for dessert.

## WINNING COMBINATIONS

*The basic considerations of pairing food and wine come down to matching the richness of the food to the body of the wine, and either contrasting or complementing the nature and intensity of the respective flavors and aromas. So much depends on your personal taste and the way the food is prepared and, as a result, the rules of wine pairing have become much more adventurous. If you're not an oenophile yourself, ask the proprietor of your local wine store (or a knowledgeable friend) for recommendations, but the pairings to the right can always be counted on to please uninitiated and sophisticated wine drinkers alike.*

| IF YOU'RE SERVING | TRY |
| --- | --- |
| Asian cuisine | Riesling |
| Beef | Cabernet Sauvignon or Shiraz |
| Chicken | White Burgundy |
| Ham | Gewürztraminer or Riesling |
| Lamb | Bordeaux, Pinot Noir, or Shiraz |
| Mexican cuisine | Rosé |
| Pasta (with cream sauce) | Chardonnay |
| Pasta (with tomato sauce) | Chianti, Barbera, or Zinfandel |
| Pork | Shiraz |
| Pizza | Pinot Grigio or Fiano di Avellino |
| Salmon | Pinot Noir (Chablis, if poached) |
| Shellfish | Sauvignon Blanc, Champagne/sparkling wine |
| Tuna | Beaujolais or Merlot |
| Turkey | Chardonnay |
| Vegetarian | Dry whites; rosé |

# Feeding vegetarians

ADVANCE NOTICE
*You'll be able to spend more time with guests if you prepare meals ahead of time. That way, you can simply heat and serve (or remove from the refrigerator) when it's time to eat.*

*Boston baked beans\**
*Beef Bourguignon*
*Chili\**
*Coq au Vin*
*Lasagne\**
*Lentil stew\**
*Macaroni and cheese\**
*Meatloaf*
*Pesto sauce (to toss with linguini)\**
*Tuscan bean soup\**
*Potato salad\**
*Quiche\**
*Tuna casserole*

*\*vegetarian; or a meal you can modify to become vegetarian*

The quickest way to offend a vegetarian is to prepare a meal and expect her to make do with the side dishes alone (say, the broccoli and mashed potatoes you serve with a roast). If you're entertaining a vegetarian guest for the first time, she or her companions should inform you of this important detail in advance, so you are able to plan an appropriate menu. Be sure to find out the exact nature of her diet—some vegetarians do eat fish, for example.

Remember that the preparation of food is as important as the content; you will need to avoid serving dishes made with chicken stock or flavored with chicken or beef bouillon cubes. Removing the meat or sausage from a tomato sauce won't render the pasta edible, nor will picking out bits of ham from a split-pea soup.

Most vegetarian guests will be delighted with any kind of pasta dish accompanied by a large salad. If you're grilling outdoors, don't forget the veggie burgers and throw on a few filling Portobello mushrooms too. If you're feeling adventurous, you could research recipes that include quinoa, a wholesome, versatile grain that has become a beloved staple of the vegetarian's diet (and is mercifully easy to prepare).

# Mushroom lasagne

*Instead of preparing a special meal for one vegetarian guest, serve everyone a great meatless lasagne. The rich texture and robust flavor of the mushrooms will satisfy the meat-eaters, and you can prepare the dish well in advance of your guests arriving, simply heating it up when it's nearly time for dinner.*

3 tablespoons/50 g butter
1 tablespoon olive oil
1 large white onion, sliced
2 garlic cloves, chopped
2 bay leaves
2¼ lbs./1 kg assorted mushrooms, sliced
1 cup/250 ml vegetable stock
1 tablespoon tomato paste/purée
12 oz./375 g pack fresh lasagne sheets
3 cups/300 g Fontina cheese, grated
½ cup/50 g Parmesan cheese, finely grated
sea salt and freshly ground black pepper

**FOR THE BÉCHAMEL SAUCE:**
3 tablespoons/50 g butter
2 tablespoons all-purpose/plain flour
¼ teaspoon freshly grated nutmeg
3 cups/750 ml whole/full-fat milk

**SERVES 8**

To make the sauce, put the butter in a saucepan set over medium heat. When it sizzles, stir in the flour and nutmeg and cook for 1 minute, stirring constantly. Remove from the heat and pour the milk into the pan, whisking constantly. Return the pan to low heat and cook for 5 minutes, stirring constantly, until the sauce is smooth and creamy.

Preheat the oven to 350°F (180°C) Gas 4. Put the butter and oil in a skillet/frying pan set over high heat and add the onion, garlic and bay leaves. Cook for 5 minutes until the onion has softened and turned opaque. Add the mushrooms, reduce the heat to

medium, and cook for 15 minutes, stirring occasionally, until the mushrooms are evenly cooked. Add the stock and tomato paste/purée and increase the heat to high. Simmer rapidly until the liquid has reduced by half. Season well with salt and pepper.

Line the bottom of an oiled baking dish with lasagne sheets. Spread over a third

of the sauce. Add one-third each of the mushrooms and grated cheese. Repeat the process and finish with a layer of lasagne. Spoon over the remaining sauce and sprinkle with the Parmesan. Bake in the preheated oven for 45 minutes, until golden brown and bubbling. Let rest for 10 minutes before serving.

ESSENTIALS

BETTER TOGETHER

*These main courses and treats are especially fun to prepare as a group.*

*Burritos and tacos*
*Dumplings*
*Empanadas*
*Fried wontons*
*From-scratch marshmallows*
*Individual pizzas*
*Jam or jelly*
*Maki rolls*
*Mini fruit pies*
*Old-fashioned taffy*
*Soft pretzels*
*Sugar cookies (with colored icing*
   *and candies for decorating)*

# Cooking for a crowd

If you're hosting a large crowd, the kinds of meals you serve require a little extra planning, because you never want to find yourself in the position of not having enough food. You'll get a lot of mileage out of roast chicken and turkey, roast beef, pot roast, and beef or pork tenderloin. Let your butcher know how many people you are feeding or, at a grocery store, estimate approximately 1 lb./450 g per person if there are bones, and ½ lb./225 g per person if the meat is boneless.

Other hearty meals that yield large quantities or are easily adjusted to yield additional servings include chili, chowders, goulash, spaghetti, and lasagne and other baked macaroni dishes. Don't forget that you can pad out meals with a large salad and a few quality loaves of bread.

# Everyone loves brownies

*Who can resist a rich, chocolatey brownie? It's an easy and elegant way to round off dinner, especially when accompanied by a good cup of coffee or a glass of dessert wine.*

4 oz./125 g unsweetened baking chocolate/plain chocolate

⅔ cup/150 g salted butter

2 cups/400 g superfine/caster sugar

1 cup/125 g all-purpose/plain flour

3 eggs

1 tablespoon pure vanilla extract

½ cup/60 g chopped walnuts (optional)

*a 9 x 12 inch/22 x 30 cm baking pan/cake tin*

**MAKES APPROXIMATELY 12**

Preheat the oven to 350°F (180°C) Gas 4 and grease the baking pan/cake tin.

Combine the chocolate and butter in a small saucepan over a low heat, stirring occasionally. Once the butter and chocolate are completely melted, remove the pan from the heat and pour the mixture into a bowl.

Gradually beat in the sugar, flour, and eggs. Stir in the vanilla and add the chopped walnuts, if desired.

Pour the brownie batter into the prepared pan/tin and bake for 25–30 minutes.

Let cool before cutting into squares.

# Sweet deal

Surely you don't need to be convinced of the importance of dessert? As you peruse potential recipes, do consider the heaviness of the preceding dinner—you might follow up a rich meal with a dessert that's equally as decadent, or counterpoint with something light and refreshing. The time of year may also inspire you (strawberry shortcake or peach cobbler in the summer, apple crisp or pumpkin cheesecake in the fall).

But if dessert really isn't your forte, don't feel any pressure to assume the role of fancy pastry chef—an elusive prospect, even for many otherwise accomplished cooks. A selection of store-bought cookies and several pints of good-quality ice cream are always appropriate, and always a sure thing.

## ELEGANT ICE CREAM

*Drizzle, scatter, or spoon on any of the options below to dress up pretty glass dishes of plain-but-perfect good-quality vanilla ice cream.*

*Angostura bitters*
*Flavored balsamic vinegar*
*Crystallized ginger*
*Candied violets or rose petals*
*Domaine de Canton liqueur*
*Fresh berries*
*Gourmet caramel topping with toasted pecans*
*Gourmet fudge sauce with walnuts*
*Mashed strawberries spiked with Chambord*
*Navan (vanilla cognac) liqueur*
*Peach or apricot preserves*

# *If you are the guest . . .*

**Always offer to help in the kitchen** Your host will probably shoo you away, but if she hands you a knife and an onion, get busy and don't worry about doing a perfect job (if she wants it done a specific way, she'll do it herself). Setting the table is always a safe task to volunteer for. If you don't know where the utensils go or how she wants the napkins folded, use your best judgment and don't make a fuss. If these details are important to your host, she'll edit your work when she has a moment.

**If you don't care for something, don't eat it** It's that simple, and your host will understand. Serving yourself an obligatory spoonful of a dish that doesn't appeal to you has become passé, and should only be exercised in the presence of very sensitive grandmothers. Don't force your child to eat anything either—no one wants to witness a weepy battle of wills over a couple of Brussels sprouts.

**Always offer to help with cleanup after meals** Your host will probably decline any dishwashing assistance, but won't mind if you help clear the table. Actually, the nicest thing you can do is to keep her company in the kitchen while she gets to work.

**If you drink more wine than the average house guest, BYOB—**don't deplete your hosts' supply the very first night!

**Don't overdo it during cocktail hour** You should be hungry by the time you sit down to dinner, not completely sloshed.

**Always find out when dinner will be served** If it's at 7 p.m., don't eat a giant lunch at 4:30. Ruining your appetite when your host has worked hard to plan and execute a meal for you is the height of thoughtlessness.

**Be punctual for all meals** If your host likes to serve a sit-down breakfast at 9 a.m., please don't roll out of bed at 11.

**Pay attention to attire** The host calls the shots, but may not say what's expected explicitly. If the majority of guests come to the breakfast table fully dressed, stop arriving in your nightgown. By the same token, if the others tend to dress nicely for dinner, you'll know to wear a sundress, not shorts.

# *Etiquette* Q & A

Q I'VE GOT A GROUP OF 12 STAYING WITH ME AND WHILE
DINNER IS ONE THING, AM I EXPECTED TO PREPARE A SIT-DOWN
BREAKFAST EACH DAY? HOW DO I GET EVERYONE TO THE TABLE
WHEN I KNOW THAT THEY'LL BE WAKING UP AT DIFFERENT TIMES
(AND NO DOUBT WANT TO EAT DIFFERENT THINGS)?

A While "French toast for 12" sounds lovely in theory, the fact is that guests aren't
expecting to be served a lavish breakfast. Certainly it would be easier to whip up a cooked-
to-order breakfast for a smaller crowd, but even this is optional. For the very reason that
everyone wakes up at different times and follows a variety of morning routines, many
hostesses simply lay out a breakfast buffet and let guests serve themselves at their leisure.
A nice buffet might include two types of pre-sliced bread, butter and a selection of jams,
cereals and granola, individual containers of yogurt, and maybe some hardboiled eggs,
along with an array of cheeses and cured meats.

Q ARE THERE ANY TACTFUL WAYS TO DEAL WITH A GUEST WHO HAS
HAD TOO MUCH TO DRINK?

A If she is accompanied by a friend, spouse, or boyfriend, alert this person to the situation
and find a solution together. You may be able to avert disaster by curbing her alcohol intake.
Discreetly offer her a cup of coffee or a big glass of water, but if she is very drunk indeed,
your mission is to get her to bed. Speak gently, acting as though nothing is wrong—a harsh
tone is likely to be met with an indignant denial of drunkenness and possibly even a
belligerent outburst. Most intoxicated guests are aware of their condition and will comply
when you suggest they lie down for a bit. A less docile guest will be reluctant to call it a
night. In this case, tell her she can rest a bit and can then rejoin the party (which, as soon
as her heads hits the pillow, is not going to happen). If the intoxicated guest has hurled
obnoxious remarks at other guests, apologize on her behalf; depending on the affront, it
may be necessary to reveal the details of the incident to the offending guest the next day
(if she does not remember) and implore her to make an additional apology.

**Q** My guests are arriving on Friday night. I'll just be getting home from work and am stressed about having to make a big dinner for everyone—I'm just going to be too tired. Is it in poor taste to order take-out food?

**A** Absolutely not. Especially if you are hosting close friends, who would never want you to overextend yourself on the first night of their stay. They'll be eager to visit with you, too, which can't happen if you're holed up in the kitchen. Ordering in or taking out food can feel leisurely, even a little hedonistic. To make this meal format extra-special, opt for exotic fare from an Indian, Thai, or Middle Eastern restaurant. Empty the contents of cartons and containers into your nicest serving bowls. Cloth napkins and candlelight will also fancy up the spread, as will a nice bottle of wine. One last concern: always pay for the food and thwart all attempts to contribute; if your guests start waving bills at you, say you'll let them pay for something else during their stay.

**Q** My fiancé and I are hosting 10 friends in my parents' country house while they're away. Because we're all young and modestly employed, is it okay to ask our guests to contribute to the cost of groceries, and share dinner prep and cleanup?

**A** Group getaways of this kind often call for splitting the check and team efforts when it comes to meals and cleanup. As de facto mistress and master of the house, you need to make the terms clear to the group—tell everyone in advance that the costs will be divided. (It may be necessary to stipulate a price cap so that no one's spending exceeds the group's comfort level.) You and your fiancé will be responsible for providing essentials such as coffee, milk, orange juice, soda, and breakfast cereal—it's very tacky to ask your guests to pay for these items. Everything else is fair game. At the end of the trip, set aside some time to figure out what everyone owes.

You and your fiancé must also delegate food prep (including picking up groceries) and cleanup responsibilities. A fun way to divide up the meals is to have the guys prepare dinner one night with the girls cleaning up, and vice versa. If you do sit-down breakfasts or lunch, each couple can trade off kitchen duties. At most gatherings of this kind, everyone is usually very conscientious and willing to do what's necessary to ensure that no one is paying or doing too much. But since it's your house, at least for the time being, you may need to nudge guests who are either oblivious of what's expected, or dragging their feet.

EXCURSIONS

IF YOU ARE HOSTING A FRIEND FROM OVERSEAS WHO DOES NOT HAVE AN
INTERNATIONAL CELL PHONE PLAN, LEND HER YOUR PHONE TO USE
DURING THE DAY WHILE YOU'RE AT WORK.

# Venturing out

When the purpose of their visit is combined with a vacation, you'll find that your guests are more independent, absolving you of the responsibility of having to entertain them every minute of the day. However, the length of stay is usually longer, possibly broken up by self-navigated day or overnight trips to see other places and people.

Whether you live in a charming seaside hamlet, an ordinary suburb, or a teeming metropolis, your guests will consider exploring the area and experiencing the local culture to be all part of the fun. You may be accustomed to the fabulous architecture, the famous museums, and the sublime vistas, but when hosting out-of-towners, you'll want to point out these unique features, organize a few outings, and generally help your guests to make the most of their stay.

## THE SURROGATE CONCIERGE

*It's pretty annoying when you ask a local in an unfamiliar city for directions or a restaurant recommendation and he replies, "I don't know." If you agree, remember that out-of-town guests are also tourists, who will be relying on your knowledge and familiarity with the area. Make sure you know the answers to all these questions:*

- *Where's a cute little place to get lunch?*
- *Where can I get a manicure?*
- *I forgot my bathing suit, where can I buy one?*
- *Where can I get a cup of coffee?*
- *If I want to go for a jog around the neighborhood, what route do you recommend?*
- *What's the best way to get to [insert major local tourist attraction, e.g. The Metropolitan Museum of Art]?*
- *Where's the nearest subway station/bus stop?*
- *How do we get onto the highway?*
- *How does public transportation to the airport work?*
- *Do you know the number of a cab company?*

# Town and country

If you live in a major tourist destination, or a city chock-full of things to see and do, invest in a few guidebooks for your guests to consult during their stay. In addition, be able to provide maps and train/bus/ferry schedules (or at least be familiar with the websites that contain this information). The week before guests arrive, pick up a few local magazines that list special events, like gallery openings, flea markets, and outdoor concerts. Most local newspapers post calendar listings—another great resource when it comes to finding out about local events and performances, including those that would be fun for children.

As the host, remember that it's important not to suggest too many outings, so that your guests don't become overwhelmed. Bear in mind that an action-packed schedule may not be your guests' cup of tea; they may prefer to lie about and do nothing, except maybe a little shopping, or hit the beach. Equally, it would be unreasonable for your guests to expect you to assume the role of tour guide. No guest should expect you to oversee their vacation experience to the point that you're the one handling every single detail. It's certainly okay to send guests on their way with some suggestions for sightseeing and a set of house keys while you stay at home or do something else with your time.

# Let's go shopping!

More than a few of your guests are bound to be passionate shoppers who consider their favorite pastime an essential part of the vacation experience. Since they will almost always contrive to work a shopping excursion into even the shortest of visits, you should be prepared to point them in the right direction, especially if you live near a major shopping destination or neighborhood (e.g. Harrods in London or Abbot Kinney Boulevard in Venice, CA).

Provide details of public transportation to local shopping hotspots, and draw on your knowledge of your guests' tastes and preferences to suggest a few boutiques that they shouldn't miss. Annotating a map will ensure that they can easily find all the stores they are hoping to visit. Include the names of any cafés or restaurants that are good pitshops—avid shoppers will certainly need to refuel.

RETAIL THERAPY
*You will already know many of the local haunts, but your guests may have other types of shopping in mind. See whether your town will be able to deliver on a request to explore these types of venues:*

*Antiques stores*
*Art galleries*
*Craft fairs*
*Department stores*
*Farmer's markets*
*Flea markets*
*Malls*
*Off-price stores*
*Outlet stores*
*Souvenir boutiques*
*Yard sales*

"TRAVELING" MOVIES
*These movies are sure to inspire wanderlust in viewers:*

*A Room with a View (1985)*
*Around the World in Eighty Days (1956)*
*The Enchanted April (1992)*
*Gentlemen Prefer Blondes (1953)*
*It Happened One Night (1934)*
*Murder on the Orient Express (1974)*
*Planes, Trains and Automobiles (1987)*
*Roman Holiday (1953)*
*Sideways (2004)*
*The African Queen (1951)*
*The Darjeeling Limited (2007)*
*To Catch a Thief (1955)*
*Two for the Road (1967)*

**ESSENTIALS**

# *Picnics*

When guests come to stay, they'll almost never expect to go on a picnic, but if you put the idea to them (and if you have the energy to organize one), no doubt they will be charmed by the proposition and eagerly agree to it. The mere mention of a picnic conjures up romantic, carefree images, from Manet's famous *Le Dejeuner sur l'Herbe* to a certain governess teaching the Von Trapp brood to sing in *The Sound of Music*. A picnic may well be the ultimate leisure activity, combining delicious, simply prepared food with beautiful scenery and a relaxed atmosphere of lighthearted games and conversations. So relaxed, in fact, that any picnicker who wishes to may feel free at any time to wander off for a nap or to simply lie down and gaze at the sky.

Choose a spot you know well that's also easily accessible. In a park, don't sacrifice seclusion for land that's uneven or soggy. The patch of beach you choose should be somewhat shielded from wind, while in the woods, figure out where the gnats and mosquitoes congregate and give those areas a wide berth. And although departing for an out-of-the-way picnic destination may appeal to you and your guests' sense of adventure, your own backyard, garden, or child's tree-house may be sufficiently "remote" and lovely.

As picnic planner in chief, you will decide how spartan or lavish the spread will be. A meal that consists of a baguette, assorted cheeses, olives, and a bottle of wine offers a satisfying mix of flavors and textures. A basket of muffins and a carafe of milk from a local dairy may tempt guests into your garden for a late-morning repast. Sandwiches constitute classic picnic fare, as does anything else you can eat with your hands— barbecued chicken, hardboiled eggs, potato chips, grapes, and strawberries also qualify. For drinks, fill up coolers with lemonade or iced tea and also bring plenty of water. Or pre-mix quantities of your favorite cocktail in a glass jar, letting the vessel do duty as both shaker and pitcher when it's time to serve.

Experienced picnickers may be eager to prepare food onsite, building a fire or setting up a portable grill. This makes hamburgers, hot dogs, chicken breasts, steaks, and grilled veggies a possibility—heartier, made-to-order fare that will turn the picnic into more of a production, but also guarantee an enthusiastic response from a hungry crowd. If this is the route you want to go, round out grilled items with at least three sides and something special for dessert, such as homemade pie.

## How to wrap a sandwich

Follow the instructions below, and your sandwiches will stay perfectly intact for you and your guests to enjoy on a picnic.

1 Tear off a rectangular sheet of wax paper about two to three times the width of the sandwich. Place the sandwich in the center of the paper.

2 Pull up the two longest ends of the paper so that they meet above the sandwich.

3 Fold these ends together, creating successive 1 in/2.5 cm folds until the sandwich is snugly wrapped.

4 Fold the remaining sides of the paper into triangles, and then tuck each triangle under the sandwich. The weight of the sandwich will keep the paper folds intact until it is time to eat, but you could also secure them with tape.

CLASSIC SANDWICHES
*Chicken salad*
*Cream cheese and jam*
*Cream cheese and smoked salmon*
*Cucumber and watercress*
*Egg salad / egg mayonnaise*
*Ham and Swiss cheese*
*Peanut butter and jelly*
*Peanut butter and marshmallow*
 *fluff*
*Roast beef and mayonnaise*
*Roasted red pepper and cheddar*
*Tomato and mozzarella*
*Tuna salad / tuna mayonnaise*

BE SURE TO HAVE LOTS OF SUNBLOCK IN YOUR MEDICINE CHEST FOR
GUESTS WHO HAVE FORGOTTEN IT. A SUNBURN CAN RUIN A WEEKEND.
A STOCKPILE OF EXTRA HATS MAY COME IN HANDY, TOO.

# Beach days

Suggesting a trip to the beach will almost always be met with an enthusiastic response—many hostesses choose to revolve entire summertime visits around days at the beach, where children are entertained, the scenery is lovely, and the mood light and easy. At a minimum, provide beach towels, a beach umbrella, and chairs (it's okay if you don't have one for each guest, as someone will always be swimming or lying down on the blanket).

You may worship the sun and prefer to spend hours at the beach, but anticipate the possibility that your guests may have a lower tolerance. Many people harbor serious concerns about skin cancer and wrinkles and need to be allowed an escape route. Be sensitive to your guests' needs—two to three hours is a reasonable time to spend at the beach. If you wish to stay longer, work out a way to get your guests home. It may be that you drive them back then return to the beach alone.

Some people enjoy eating picnic-style on the beach, others don't (too sandy!). Snacks are less important than drinks; bring plenty of water. Alcohol is often not permitted and is probably a bad idea anyway.

If guests with children are unfamiliar with the basics of beach etiquette, you may need to remind them that sand-throwing, running near other people's blankets, and tossing a football near sunbathers are all anathema to courteous beach-goers. Child safety—both in and out of the water—is also crucial. Parents need to be extra-vigilant, which may be challenging if there are chatty adults around to distract them, and when the general atmosphere at the beach is so carefree.

**ESSENTIALS**

IN THE BEACH BAG
*Bandana or headscarf*
*Beach towels (at least two)*
*Blanket or quilt*
*Books and magazines*
*Bottled water*
*Camera*
*Cute cover-up, kaftan, or sarong*
*Flip-flops, espadrilles, or*
   *huaraches*
*Hair elastics*
*Leave-in conditioner*
*Moisturizing lip balm (SPF 15)*
*Straw hat*
*Sunglasses*
*Sunscreen—a hardcore one*
   *(SPF 30 and up) for face, and*
   *a lighter formula (SPF 15*
   *and below) for body*

# *If you are the guest...*

**If you're lucky enough** to have friends and family who live in, or near, a major travel destination, research the sights you'd like to see and the restaurants you'd like to experience before you arrive. Your host will furnish you with basic directions and information about public transportation, but make an attempt to pay attention to, and familiarize yourself with, your surroundings when you're out and about. This way, you won't be starting from scratch every time you leave the house.

**If your host chooses to join you** for sightseeing or on jaunts into town, pay for small incidental purchases like water, coffee, and snacks. This is very "I'm being a good guest" behavior, and an especially great way to show your appreciation to a host who won't let you lift a finger to help her out at home.

**If you are staying longer than a week,** volunteering to spend a night or two at a hotel—to give your hosts a break—is a lovely gesture. Look at this respite as an opportunity to explore a different neighborhood or to splurge on top-rated accommodations. After all, you've saved so much money by staying with friends—treat yourself!

**If you're staying longer than two days,** expect to dine out one night during your stay. If your hosts are the same age as, or younger than you, expect to pay the check.

**Be conscientious about paying your host back** for any tickets (theater, ballet, concert...) she may have purchased in advance for you to enjoy during your stay. If she has done so without consulting you, act as though you're thrilled (even if you're not).

**When it comes to beach outings,** picnics, sailing, and other outdoor diversions, it's absolutely fine to opt out. It is not okay, however, to join the group and then complain about the weather, wind, difficult terrain, or bugs.

"IN SHORT, EVEN IF YOU ARE NOT AT ALL AN OUTDOOR TYPE OF WOMAN AT HEART, YOU SHOULD AT LEAST DRESS THE PART WHEN YOU SPEND THE WEEKEND IN THE COUNTRY, AND BY ALL MEANS, LEAVE YOUR FALSE EYELASHES IN TOWN." *from* A Guide to Elegance *(1964) by Genevieve Antoine Dariaux*

# *Etiquette* Q & A

Q My sister and her family are coming to stay and we definitely want to carve out some adult time—perhaps dinner or a movie on one or two of the nights. We don't have any kids of our own but have been charged with the task of hiring a babysitter. Where do I find one, and who pays?

A Tackle this task at least two weeks before the dates you're thinking of booking, especially if they fall on a Friday or Saturday night. Any of your friends who have children will be able to recommend reliable candidates; you might also check out the forums on neighborhood websites for names and resources.

These are also the proper channels to consult when it comes to determining an appropriate hourly rate, which may or may not be the same as where your guests live. Increase this rate slightly if there is more than one child. You should also take into account the babysitter's level of experience; a part-time professional nanny trying to clock some extra hours should always be paid more than a high-school student.

Technically, it's the parents' responsibility to pay, not yours, especially since you are already incurring expenses to host them in the first place. However, it would be kind of you to offer to split the babysitter's fee, particularly if you are the one who has suggested going out, or if you suspect it would be appreciated financially.

Q I'M HOSTING A FRIEND WHO LOVES NIGHTLIFE IN A HUGE WAY. WITH HER, A SATURDAY NIGHT OUT CAN EASILY LAST UNTIL 3 A.M., AND I OFTEN HAVE TROUBLE KEEPING UP AND STAYING UP. IS IT TERRIBLY RUDE IF, AFTER DINNER AND A FEW DRINKS, I LEAVE HER OUT ON HER OWN?

A With a chance to spend an evening or two in a fabulous city with an equally fabulous nightlife, your friend will probably want to party with a little more gusto than usual and be especially keen to pursue every adventure that comes her way. Try to understand this, and no matter how tired you are, push yourself to last an hour or two beyond your comfort level.

Guests are supposed to defer to the host's rhythms and lifestyle, so your friend should join you when you're ready to go—it's obviously never a good idea to leave a friend alone in a bar, dance hall, or at a house party, especially in an unfamiliar city. If you've gone out with a group and your friend either knows the others well, or appears to feel comfortable with some or all of these people, it's okay for you to duck out, as long as she has a set of house keys to let herself in (whenever that happens to be).

ACTIVITIES

# Just have fun!

Proposing any activities to your dearest friends and family members beyond sitting around talking and laughing, and cooking and eating meals, may not be necessary. Other guests, however, may require constant stimulation. A few carefully chosen activities will enrich your guests' visit, pass the time if boredom should descend on the group, and also have the potential to create new memories you can all recall the next time you get together. The activities you suggest will, of course, depend on whether you have boundless amounts of time and energy to plan them, or the bare minimum required. Fortunately, the possibilities range from taxing and time-consuming to blissfully lowkey.

If you're hosting children, you'll find that structured activities will keep them occupied for longer periods of time and facilitate play with your own children, if anyone's feeling antisocial or shy. Seasonal activities, such as carving pumpkins in the fall, cutting out paper snowflakes in winter, and staging a lemonade stand during the warm summer months (see page 93), are easy to plan.

# A lemonade stand

A perfect summer day will see bikers heading out for rides, hikers hitting the trail, and neighbors blithely meandering their way to the market on foot. These factors, combined with the beautiful weather, create the perfect conditions for setting up a lemonade stand—an engrossing, even educational activity for children ages five and up.

Many items can masquerade as a lemonade stand—a large, sturdy cardboard box, a card table, milk crate, or apple bushel, or a toy chest. You might also consider selling snacks like granola bars or popcorn, or combining the lemonade effort with a full-on bake sale. Cookies and other baked goodies are hard to resist, especially when a small, smiling face is imploring you to buy some.

## Fresh lemonade

*Quick and easy to prepare, this old-fashioned homemade lemonade is tangy and refreshing.*

6 lemons
6 cups / 1.5 litres water
1 cup / 225 g sugar
fresh mint leaves, to garnish (optional)

**MAKES ABOUT 2 QUARTS / LITRES**

Roll the lemons firmly on the countertop a few times—this breaks up the pulp and means they will release more juice. Now squeeze the lemons to obtain about one cup of juice.

In a large saucepan, combine the water and sugar. Heat slowly until the sugar melts, stirring occasionally (an adult should supervise this process). Allow the sugar mixture to cool.

Pour the sugar mixture and lemon juice into a large plastic pitcher. Stir, and add water to taste.

Chill and serve over ice, adding the fresh mint leaves (if using).

## SETTING UP

The stand can be erected on the front lawn—clearly visible to customers, but near enough for you to keep a close eye on things. And if business is good, the children can easily run inside to make more lemonade.

**Cover the stand** with festive fabric or a tablecloth. Work with the kids to create a large sign to prop against the stand. Make sure the letters—especially the word "LEMONADE"—are large and visible from a distance. Hang smaller signs around the neighborhood to drum up thirsty customers. Set up a CD player and play upbeat music to keep the kids stimulated and alert. Keep the cups and napkins in a small box behind the stand so they can't blow away or get dirty.

**Pricing the lemonade** at 25 cents/25 pence a glass will make it easy for the kids to do the financial calculations on their own. Be sure to give them some bills and coins so they can make change. Instruct them to keep this box tucked away behind the stand.

**Keep a pitcher of ice water** and a bowl of extra sugar handy for customers who want to adjust the sweetness of their drink.

## HANDY TIPS

*Be sure the stand is easily accessible, and visible, but that it is not blocking any driveways or mailboxes.*

*If the stand is set up in the sun, bring out a large beach umbrella to provide shade. Be sure the children wear sunscreen and reapply every two hours.*

*Keep well within earshot of the children so you can lend a hand if necessary.*

*If business is slow the children may get bored—have lawn games or coloring books handy to keep them entertained.*

*Instruct the children that they should greet all customers with a smile—but that they should never leave the "stand zone" unaccompanied by an adult to approach a stranger, especially if he or she is in a car.*

*Take down all the signs and clean up once the children are done selling for the day.*

# Fun for everyone

Lots of activities have multigenerational appeal. For example, you could set up a crafts table outdoors and have each guest create a page to compile in a guest book, providing patterned paper, stickers, glitter, and magic markers. Or consider tie-dying T-shirts (in a variety of sizes); a project that will yield a unique keepsake for your guests to use and enjoy long after the visit. The supplies you'd need for this project, like rubber bands and fabric dye, are inexpensive and easy to find.

In a pinch, never underestimate the power of posing silly riddles to one another, telling hair-raising ghost stories, or rigging up a karaoke machine. Why not take a cue from Jane Austen's *Mansfield Park* and assign everyone parts of a play to read aloud? Encouraging the kids to stage their own short concert or dance performance would be a charming form of entertainment, too.

A STROLL AROUND THE NEIGHBORHOOD OR A SLIGHTLY MORE STRENUOUS TREK THROUGH A NEARBY PARK IS A GREAT WAY TO WORK OFF THE PREVIOUS EVENING'S MEAL. WALKING IS THE KIND OF EXERCISE THAT FEELS MORE SOCIAL THAN ATHLETIC, BUT AFTER 30 MINUTES OF WALKING AT A LEISURELY PACE, THE AVERAGE WOMAN HAS BURNED ABOUT 100—150 CALORIES.

# Outdoor options

When the weather is nice, your own backyard may offer a wellspring of potential activities, from jumping into the pool for a swim to tackling a gardening project as a group. Alternatively, you might propose a walk in your local park or in a nearby forest or meadow; or how about a sight-seeing city tour?

Exercise will likely be central to some guests' idea of the perfect getaway. You might want to join them on a stroll or a jog around the neighborhood. Team sports may be another way to go; remind guests to bring the appropriate shoes and equipment if you're planning to propose an exhilarating hike, or a game of golf or tennis. If bike riding is on the agenda, encourage guests to bring their cycles with them (or figure out the particulars of renting them locally).

HOW TO THROW
A FRISBEE™
*An impromptu game of frisbee is a fun way to round off a picnic or trip to the park. Once you have mastered the basic technique (given below), it's a matter of practice makes perfect.*

1 *Grip the disc by placing your middle and index fingers along the inside rim, and your thumb on the outside rim.*

2 *Stand so that your feet are shoulder-width apart.*

3 *If you are right-handed, hold the disc horizontally, and cross your arm in front of you, positioning the Frisbee™ on the left side of your body (lefties, do the opposite). Twist your body so your throwing arm is slightly behind you.*

4 *Holding onto the disc, rotate your wrist slightly, and then snap your wrist forward, as you un-twist your body. Release the disc at the point when your arm has reached a 45-degree angle in front of you.*

# Anyone for croquet?

Lawn games have a quaint, nostalgic appeal, so when you suggest them, do so with a wink and a smile. Croquet is a classic—easy to play, only mildly competitive, and conducive to carrying on conversations as you make your way around the lawn. And, since the balls are so colorful, and look so pretty in lush, green grass, you'll want to take advantage of this picturesque photo opportunity.

## SETTING UP

For optimal play, select an area on the lawn that's not too bumpy and where the grass is short. The croquet "court" should be 100 feet long and 50 feet wide/30 metres long and 15 metres wide, but you can adjust the size to fit in a smaller area. Nine wickets are arranged in a "double diamond pattern" with a stake at either end. The stake on the north end of the course is the turning stake—which indicates that players must now move in the opposite direction—and a finishing stake, which ends the game, on either end.

## PLAYERS

Two teams, four balls (blue, black, red, and yellow). One team plays with the blue and black balls; the other team plays with the red and yellow balls. Play order: Blue, red, black, yellow.

## OBJECT

Players must advance their ball through the course by hitting them with their mallet. Players score one point for each wicket they pass through and stake they tap in the correct order. The first side to score 14 wicket points and 2 stake points for each ball wins.

## RULES

- Each time a player scores, or taps the "turning stake," she earns an extra turn. If the player hits another player's ball with her own ball she earns two extra shots.

- If you hit your ball past a wicket without scoring you must return it to its original position.

- Players who complete the course can remain in the game as "rovers." They may "roquet" (use their ball to strike an opponent's ball) any balls in play, but may only hit their ball once per turn, and cannot roquet a ball twice in succession.

# Get your skates on

During a wintertime visit, someone is bound to suggest the idea of ice-skating, a sport that can be enjoyed by all ages, and in virtually any setting, whether it's a municipal skating rink in a big city or a frozen-over pond in the country. (Don't forget to inspect the pond closely and to test the thickness of the ice in several different places using a cordless drill. The ice should be between four and a half and seven inches/12–18 cm deep to be safe for skating.) If you're hosting a large group, there is likely to be at least one beginner in your midst, in which case the following tips may come in handy:

1 Skates are comprised of two sections: the boot and the blade. The jagged area at the tip of the blade is called a "toe pick;" the toe pick can serve as your "brake" when skating backwards.

2 Walk around in your skates a bit to get used to them. If your skates feel too tight or loose, either retie them or try another size.

3 When stepping onto the ice for the first time, step out sideways; this prevents your skates from slipping out from under you.

4 Take small steps with your blades pointing outward to propel yourself forward. Bring each skate to the center after every step to maintain your balance. To stop, create a triangle with your skates, toes together, heels out.

5 When moving around the rink, keep your knees slightly bent and rest your weight on the balls of your feet. Hold your arms slightly out to the side to maintain balance.

6 If you slip, avoid using your arms to break your fall. Instead, bend your knees and lean backwards so you land on your bottom.

7 To get back up, place your hands and knees on the ice. Move each foot directly under you so you are in a crouching position. From here, stand up as you normally would.

# Three classic card games

Gathering at a table to play cards continues to be a universally appealing way to spend an hour or two. You might suggest this to your guests as a way to keep the party going after dinner—and if you're hosting a particularly competitive, card-savvy crowd, go ahead and organize a bridge or pinochle "tournament" as the evening's main event.

On the other hand, some card games are appropriately lowkey, a one-on-one activity that can instantly perk up spirits on a dark, rainy afternoon, or take the place of conversation when you've temporarily run out of things to say. Another plus: For the most part, card games are an activity that guests of all ages can participate in (just use candy or pennies when playing poker with kids).

### FIVE-CARD DRAW POKER
**Number of players: 2–8**

1 Players ante up—they place the same amount of money or tokens into the pot before the game begins.

2 Each player is dealt five cards, one at a time, facedown.

3 Players may now bet, starting from the dealer's left. Players may also choose to fold—discard their hand and sit out—at this time.

4 After bets are placed, the remaining players may discard one to three cards and receive new ones.

5 Another round takes place. Players can fold, raise the bet, or "check." If a player checks, the next player can raise the current bet; afterward, all players must either match that bet or fold. The player who checked must now match the current bet and "call," forcing all players to show their hands.

6 The game ends when there are no more raises. The highest-ranking hand wins the pot. If all players but one choose to fold, the remaining player does not need to reveal his hand.

## SIMPLE GIN RUMMY
Number of players: 2

1 Each player is dealt ten cards, one at a time. The dealer starts the discard pile by placing one card face up—called the "upcard." The remaining cards, known as the "stock," are placed facedown in the stock pile.

2 Players organize their hand into "melds"—sets of three or four cards of the same rank—or runs (a sequence of three or four cards in a given suit).

3 At the start of each turn, players may either select the upcard from the discard pile or the top card from the stock pile. After making their selection, they must then discard a card, face up, on top of the upcard.

4 The round continues until one of the players calls "Gin"—he may do this only when all of his cards fit into melds. The player who calls "Gin" first, and has the cards to back it up, wins.*

5 Cards are gathered up and shuffled; then, a new hand is dealt to each player. Play continues until one of the players wins five rounds.

*You can try to prevent your opponent from calling "Gin" before you by knocking (but only do this if you suspect she has more "deadwood"—cards that don't fit into any melds—than you do). When a player knocks, both players must lay out all of their melds on the table. Your opponent now has the opportunity to "lay off" any cards that fit into your melds, in an attempt to reduce her deadwood. Ultimately, the player with the fewest number of deadwood cards wins the round.

## CRAZY EIGHTS
Number of players: 2+

1 The dealer deals five cards, one at a time, to each player. The remaining cards are placed facedown in the center of the table as stock. The top card is placed face up next to these cards to start the discard pile.

2 Play moves clockwise around the table, with players discarding their cards one by one. The discarded card must either match the suit or rank of the discard pile's top card. The fun part: Any eight may be played on any card; when a player throws down an eight, he calls out the next suit to be played.

3 If a player cannot match the suit or rank of the top card, and has no eight to play, he must take a card from the stock pile.

4 The first person to get rid of all of their cards wins.

# *Parlor games*

The Victorians were mad about parlor games, and people still like to play them today, especially on rainy days or after dinner (first equipped with bowls of ice cream and additional glasses of wine). The following are games that require no equipment (except for pen and paper on occasion), but do require quick thinking, a sense of humor and, depending on the game, a certain amount of irreverence!

## CHARADES
A great, goofy classic that guests of all ages will enjoy.

### How to play
Divide your group into two teams. On strips of paper, each team member should write down either the title of a book, a movie, or a television show. Throw the strips of paper into a hat or a bowl; players must close their eyes and pull out one of these strips of paper at random.

Now, each player must provide non-verbal* clues to help her fellow team members to guess the title correctly. First, convey what genre the title falls into by miming a movie camera, a book, or a television set. Once this is established, the most common clues include the number of words in the title, as well as the word you are currently acting out (both indicated by holding up the corresponding number of fingers); "sounds like" (hold your hand up to your ear and then point to something in the room or act out the word); and whether or not the word in question is a big word (like "adventure") or a small word (like "the" or "and").

To make play more exciting and difficult, set a time limit and have someone record the number of guesses it takes a team to determine each title—you can compare these numbers at the end of each round to determine which team has won.

*A review of the codes for these non-verbal clues may be helpful at the start as different guests may be used to their own versions of the game. Like all parlor games, the rules can vary.

## Six degrees of Kevin Bacon

A brain-wracking trivia game that is based on the idea that any actor can be linked to the actor Kevin Bacon by six degrees or fewer (that is, six other actors by way of the films these actors have appeared in).

### How to play

Divide your group into two teams. One team selects an actor and the rival team must consider the movies this actor has starred in until they arrive at a route that ultimately leads to a Kevin Bacon movie. The shorter the route, the better.

### Example: Jane Fonda

Fonda was in *Barefoot in the Park* (1967) with Robert Redford, who was in *Out of Africa* (1985) with Meryl Streep, who was in *The River Wild* (1994) with Kevin Bacon. Number of degrees: three.

Scoring is optional, but to determine a winner, you would time the rounds and tally the number of degrees per actor challenge.

A variation of this game would be to choose two actors at random (unlikely pairings—say Sir Anthony Hopkins and Dolly Parton—make the task more challenging) and try to link them by six degrees or fewer.

## Two truths and a lie

This is a great ice-breaker if your guests don't know each other well. But be warned—this game can also become a trifle risqué and provocative, especially at a coed gathering.

### How to play

Each guest must make three statements about herself—two that are true and one that is false. Upon hearing these statements, the rest of the group must guess the one that is a lie. Once the "judges" choose a statement, the "liar" must reveal the statement that is false. You can turn this into a drinking game by making the liar drink if the judges identify the lie correctly; the judges must drink if they get it wrong.

# *If you are the guest...*

**Be a good sport** Literally, be "game for anything." If some guests want to play a board or parlor game and others are dragging their feet, be the guest who changes their mind—don't be the guest who sides with the naysayers.

**Your host needs downtime** Don't be offended if she disappears to her bedroom for a quick nap. This would be a good time for you to get out of the house and go for a walk, run, or bike ride.

**Go with the flow** The visit can't be all on your terms; you should defer to the host's plans and ideas and adjust to her rhythms. If you're the type who can't sit still, find some sort of solitary activity to divert you—don't try to organize a dodgeball tournament or volunteer to make a huge breakfast for everyone without seeing whether your host has something else in mind. Guests who try to "take over" in this manner cause their hosts certain distress and may put the kibosh on future invitations.

**Always act like you're having a good time** A bad attitude or a long face will quickly identify you as the weekend's wet blanket and, consequently, the weekend's pariah.

**When it comes to taking part** in competitive games and sports, be a good loser. Don't let a trouncing on the tennis court affect your mood during dinner.

# *Etiquette* Q & A

Q I'M WORRIED THAT ONE OF OUR GUESTS ISN'T HAVING A
GOOD TIME——SHE NEVER WANTS TO JOIN IN ANY ACTIVITIES, FOR
EXAMPLE WHEN THE REST OF OUR GROUP WENT CROSS-COUNTRY
SKIING THE OTHER DAY, OR EVEN WHEN WE WENT OUTSIDE IN
THE BACKYARD AND HAD A SNOWMAN-MAKING CONTEST.
HOW CAN I GET HER TO PARTICIPATE?

A Respect the fact that she may not be an outdoorsy type—it's not uncommon for
a "city mouse" to feel like a fish out of water in the country. She may just need some
reassurance that she won't be stranded during your treks into the wilderness, and that it's
okay if she participates at her own pace. Then again, it may be that she just doesn't like
the cold! Whatever her reasons, don't pressure her if she seems truly adamant, and it
would be very unkind and passive aggressive to draw attention to her decision to opt out
(or whisper about it to someone else behind her back). Always appear flexible, even if
you are disappointed by her lack of enthusiasm. Instead of trying to convince your guest,
suggest a few alternative activities that may be of interest to her. And if the "activity"
that most appeals to her happens to be curling up on the couch with a book, so be it.

Q MY GUESTS' KIDS ARE NOT PLAYING NICELY WITH MY
KIDS. FRANKLY, THEIR BEHAVIOR IN GENERAL LEAVES MUCH
TO BE DESIRED. HOW DO I DEAL WITH THIS TACTFULLY?

A Voice your concerns to the children's parents and let them address the problem.
When a more immediate reproach is required and the parents aren't around to react
appropriately, you're in charge. This means that you have the right to object to certain
behaviors—try the pat reprimand "In our house, we don't [insert offending behavior
here]." It's courteous, reasonable, but effectively firm.

Q I KEEP SUGGESTING POSSIBLE ACTIVITIES TO MY GUESTS, EVERYTHING FROM BOWLING TO SKIING AT A NEARBY RESORT, BUT THEY'RE RELUCTANT BECAUSE OF THE COST INVOLVED. WHAT ACTIVITIES CAN I SUGGEST TO THEM THAT ARE INEXPENSIVE OR FREE?

A Many more than you think. Local newspapers and magazines are quick to point out free and affordable entertainment to their readers—peruse these listings for some unique options. Other ideas: Check out a sporting event at a local high school or university. You could also organize a nature walk, or even a neighborhood scavenger hunt. And for a fun nighttime activity, locate some sky charts online, print them out, and try to find constellations as you gaze at the stars (toast some marshmallows, too).

Q LAST NIGHT, I WAS HANGING OUT WITH MY COUSIN'S KIDS AND TOLD THEM THEY COULD WATCH A DVD THEY SPOTTED ON MY BOOKSHELF. LITTLE DID I KNOW THAT THIS MOVIE WOULD BE CONSIDERED UNSUITABLE BY MY COUSIN AND HER HUSBAND. NOW WATCHING THIS MOVIE IS ALL THE KIDS CAN TALK ABOUT, AND WORLD WAR III IS ABOUT TO BEGIN. WHAT CAN I DO RECTIFY THE SITUATION?

A Lesson learned, right? There's nothing you can do in this situation but let your cousin and her husband sort this out. A good rule of thumb when suggesting activities to little ones is to run anything you have in mind by the parents first. If the kids themselves ask you if they may do something always say, "Sure we can do that, but only if it's okay with your mom and dad."

DEPARTURES

# *Exit strategies*

When you're still in the throes of enjoying each other's company, it can be difficult to bring up the subject of your guests' departure. But there are a few details you'll need to address, so that your guests can leave your home with little last-minute drama or stress.

First, determine what time they would like to leave and advise them on the most direct route out of town, or on the mode of public transportation that will take them to the airport or train station (if you're not driving them there yourself). When you know what time your guests wish to leave, suggest a wake-up time and ask what they would like for breakfast. Offer to pack a lunch, or snacks, for your guests to take with them so that they don't have to spend money on food during their journey (and will have the chance to enjoy last night's brownies one more time).

IT IS EQUALLY OFFENSIVE TO SPEED A GUEST WHO WOULD LIKE TO STAY AND TO DETAIN ONE WHO IS ANXIOUS TO LEAVE. *Homer*

# Fond farewells

The day before your guests are scheduled to leave, offer to do a load of laundry for them, so that they don't have to cart home suitcases full of dirty clothes. Write out recipe cards for any dishes you prepared for them that they enjoyed and, if you have a guest book, urge them to sign it if they haven't done so already.

On the morning of their departure, good guests should always ask if they should strip the bed or make it. If they don't ask, it's okay to give them instructions—tell them if they should leave the sheets in a heap on the bed, place them in a clothes hamper, or transfer them to the laundry room. Collect any books that they have borrowed from you, and track down those you would like to lend them for their journey home. Some hosts like to give their guests farewell gifts—nothing over the top, but vegetables from the garden, a box of locally made sweets, postcards, or a jar of homemade jam are all lovely, packable keepsakes.

" 'SEEING THE GUEST OFF' IS AN ESSENTIAL POINT OF HOSPITALITY...IF THE HOST IS SEEING THE GUEST OFF, HE USUALLY GOES WITH THE GUEST, PARTICULARLY A WOMAN GUEST, AS FAR AS THE AUTOMOBILE. IN A CITY APARTMENT HOUSE, THIS RESPONSIBILITY ENDS WHEN THE GUEST HAS GOT INTO THE ELEVATOR..." *From* Vogue's Book of Etiquette *(1948) by Millicent Fenwick*

# *If you are the guest...*

Write and send a thank-you note. Even if the hostess is your sister or your best friend of many years, formally acknowledging her hospitality is a mandatory gesture, according to the annals of good etiquette. But don't send a note for propriety's sake alone—do it because she's probably not expecting one. So when she does receive your note—handwritten on pretty stationery, please—it will brighten her day and gladden her heart. Knowing how appreciative you are will make her feel happy that she invited you and will certainly guarantee your being invited to stay again.

**Here's a rundown of the essential components:**
1  Begin with an enthusiastic expression of gratitude.
2  Mention specific details of the visit that made an impression on you.
3  Acknowledge anything you did that may have been slightly annoying (e.g. "Sorry Emma barked so much" or "Sorry I kept using up all of the hot water").
4  Make much of any show of hospitality that was above and beyond gracious (e.g. "It was so unbelievably kind of you to drive us to and from the airport" or "Thank you for handling the details of our day trip to the Grand Canyon— we never would have made it there if it weren't for your careful planning").
5  Reiterate your gratitude in closing.

Dear Belinda,

Thank you so much for letting me stay the weekend with you while I was in town for my cousin's wedding. Your apartment is adorable! And you were such a wonderful hostess, from the delicious café lattes you served me in the morning (I'm dying for one right now!) to helping me figure out train schedules and even letting me raid your closet for something fabulous to wear to the rehearsal dinner! I only wish that my family obligations hadn't prevented me from spending as much time with you as I would have liked. Hopefully the next visit will be much longer and less stressful—maybe at my place in L.A.? I would love to have you, if only to reciprocate your wonderful hospitality. Thanks again for everything and I hope to talk to you very soon.

Much love,
Abby

Dear Mrs. Hendricks,

Thank you for hosting me at your lovely beach house! Robert is so fond of the Vineyard—I know it's a very special place for you and your family and I feel very lucky to have had the chance to experience it for a few days. From waking up to the smell of your fabulous cinnamon rolls to falling asleep to the sounds of crashing waves, every moment was absolutely delightful. Especially the clambake Saturday night! That was such a special treat, thank you for taking the time to put that together. Oh, and Robert and I loved the local theater's production of As You Like It. It was so nice of you to get us all tickets to see it. Thank you again for a wonderful time. I hope you and Mr. Hendricks enjoy the rest of your summer!

Fondly,
Marjorie

# *Etiquette* Q & A

Q I HAVE A VERY EARLY MEETING AT WORK WHICH MEANS
I WILL HAVE TO LEAVE THE HOUSE BEFORE MY GUESTS DO.
IS IT OKAY IF I'M NOT THERE TO SEE THEM OFF PERSONALLY?

A Yes—busy schedules often get in the way of one's ability to fulfill the obligations of classic hospitality and you shouldn't worry about it too much at all. Say your goodbyes the night before; this would also be the time to review driving directions, or how best to access the airport or train station via taxi or mass transit.

Remember to review the particulars of locking up the house. Many doors lock automatically, others require manually turning a key. If this is the case, discuss how the keys are to be returned—slid beneath the door, placed under a doormat, or the inside of a mailbox are all popular hiding places. Failing that, your guests could mail your keys back to you. To be safe, ask them to mail the package to your place of business, not your home address.

Finally, the next morning, leave a lovely farewell note; include anything you forgot to mention the night before and the numbers where you can be reached until they are on their way.

Q I HAD SUCH A GOOD TIME HOSTING MY FRIENDS; I ONLY
GET TO SEE THEM ONCE OR TWICE A YEAR AND I'M FEELING
BLUE NOW THEY'RE GONE. WHAT CAN I DO TO GET OVER IT?

A Wonderfully exciting, laughter-filled experiences are almost always accompanied
by a "let down" afterward. These feelings of sadness are normal—most people have a
hard time saying goodbye to dear friends and family that they don't get to see very often,
and it can be hard to return to your comparatively lackluster daily routine. One way to
counteract these temporary doldrums is to spend some time with the photos you took
during your guests' visit. If you've ever spent time uploading and organizing digital
photos on a photo-sharing website, you know that it takes up a lot of time and mental
energy. And it feels good to relive those moments. You might choose to have some of
these photos printed—to send to your guests and/or to mount in a scrapbook.

Another way to comfort yourself is to get in touch with your departed guests when they
get home; together you can nail down a date in the future that would be convenient for
you all to get together again. Having such a date in place always makes a beloved
guest's absence that much easier to bear.

Q I'VE JUST HOSTED FRIENDS AT MY IN-LAWS' COUNTRY HOUSE
AND WOULD PREFER THAT MY GUESTS ADDRESS THANK-YOU NOTES
TO THEM—NOT MY HUSBAND AND ME—SINCE THEY WERE KIND
ENOUGH TO LET US ALL USE IT WHILE THEY WERE AWAY. HOW DO I
GET THIS POINT ACROSS WITHOUT SEEMING PRESUMPTUOUS OR BOSSY?

A If you are close with these guests and they know you to be a stickler in the manners
department, they'll have considered this detail already and asked for your in-laws' address
accordingly. If you're worried that the inclination to write a thank-you note—even to you, let
alone your in-laws—might be lost on certain guests, you can overcompensate for this gaffe by
being extremely effusive in your own thank-you note, and perhaps sending an especially nice
thank-you gift. Alternatively, you should feel no qualms about writing a follow-up email the next
day, to thank your guests for coming—and to mention casually that you're going to be writing a
note to your in-laws and have included their address if anyone would like to do the same.

# Picture credits

Images taken from Japanese
Patterns, published by
The Pepin Press,
www.pepinpress.com
Pages 4–5 background, 9,
13r, 14l, 17r, 20r, 22–23,
25, 26l, 29r, 32r, 33r, 34–
35, 37, 45r, 46l, 57r, 60l,
62l, 65r, 68–69, 71, 73r,
74l, 77r, 78l, 81r, 83r, 86–
87, 89, 95r, 96l, 99l, 111r,
114–115, 117, 119r, 121r,
124–125, endpapers

## PHOTOGRAPHY

© Photolibrary Group:
Pages 94, 101

Caroline Arber
Pages 3, 28, 32b, 41,
72/designed and made by
Jane Cassini and Ann
Brownfield, 76/Sharland &
Lewis
(www.sharlandandlewis.com)

Jan Baldwin
Page 12bl

Martin Brigdale
Pages 52, 57r, 80a, 80bl, 81

David Brittain
Pages 40, 90bl

Peter Cassidy
Pages 29l, 36, 38br, 45r,
66a, 66b, 80br, 103a

Jean Cazals
Page 121

Vanessa Davies
Pages 93r, 97b both

Christopher Drake
Pages 4l/an apartment in
Milan designed by Daniela
Micol Wajskol, interior
designer
(danielaw@tiscalinet.it), 73,
78r, 83c,103c

Dan Duchars
Pages 90a, 98, 116, 120,
123

Chris Everard
Page 113

Michelle Garrett
Page 33

Catherine Gratwicke
Page 118

Winfried Heinze
Pages 10c, 10b, 12br, 13,
15al, 17 both, 20c, 21, 29r

Andrea Jones
Page 103b

Richard Jung
Pages 42 background, 61,
64, 65 both, 92, 93l, 95

Sandra Lane
Page 19

Tom Leighton
Page 18bl

William Lingwood
Pages 30l, 30r, 46, 48 both,
50, 51, 53, 54, 104–107,
110, 111

Paul Massey
Page 16/Michael Giannelli
& Greg Shano's home in
East Hampton

Diana Miller
Page 32a

David Montgomery
Page 20a

David Munns
Page 60l

Noel Murphy
Pages 6al, 6br, 44, 66c

Kristin Perers
Page 112a

Claire Richardson
Pages 84b, 96l, 119

Debi Treloar
Pages 2, 5l, 6ar, 6bl, 26, 27,
31, 38a, 38bl, 39, 42 inset,
45l, 55, 56, 57l, 58, 59, 62
both, 63, 67, 70, 75al, 75bl,
78l inset, 79, 82, 83l, 83r,
112b

Simon Upton
Page 102/Lena Proudlock
(www.lenaproudlock.com)

Ian Wallace
Pages 1, 43, 47, 60r, 84c, 85

Alan Williams
Pages 12a/the Norfolk home
of Geoff & Gilly Newberry of
Bennison Fabrics, all fabrics
by Bennison
(www.bennisonfabrics.com),
77l, 84a, 109

Polly Wreford
Pages 4r/Hilary Robertson and
Alistair McGowan, Hastings,
5r, 8/Mary Foley's house in
Connecticut, 10a, 11, 15ar,
15b/Sasha Waddell's home
available from
www.beachstudios.co.uk,
18br, 20b, 24, 32c, 77r, 88,
90br, 91, 93c, 96r, 97a, 99,
112c, 128

# Recipe credits

Fiona Beckett
St Clement's punch

Susannah Blake
Toasted bagels with cream
cheese and smoked salmon

Linda Collister
Lemon, almond, and
blueberry muffins

Ross Dobson
Mushroom lasagne

Louise Pickford
Hot buttered rum

Ben Reed
Bellini
Bloody Mary
Blue blazer
Brandy Alexander
Cosmopolitan
Cuba libre
Daiquiri
Flirtini
French 75
Gimlet
Hot toddy
Irish coffee
Kir royale
Mai Tai
Manhattan
Margarita
Martini
Mojito
Pimm's
Piña colada
Sidecar

Fran Warde
Granola
Mulled wine

# UK sources

**The Atlantic Blanket Company**
0845 6585194
www.atlanticblankets.com
*Gorgeous blankets and throws.*

**The Board Game Company**
www.boardgamecompany.co.uk
*Family and party board games
as well as jigsaw puzzles.*

**Cologne & Cotton**
Visit
www.cologneandcotton.com
for details of your nearest store.
*Elegant bed linen, pretty
towels and home fragrances.*

**The Conran Shop**
Michelin House
81 Fulham Road
London SW3 6RD
020 7589 7401
www.conran.com
*Stylish glassware, cocktail
equipment, china, bedding
and bath treats.*

**Designers Guild**
261–271 & 275–277
King's Road
London SW3 5EN
020 7351 5775
www.designersguild.com
*Bold and beautiful fabrics,
rugs and blankets, as well as
ceramics and candle holders.*

**Dibor**
www.dibor.com
*Traditional French china and
glassware, and striped linen
tea towels.*

**Habitat**
Visit www.habitat.co.uk for
details of your nearest store.
*Stylish, inexpensive
glassware, tableware and
bed linen.*

**Heal's**
196 Tottenham Court Road
London W1P 9LD
Call 020 7896 7451 or visit
www.heals.co.uk for details
of your nearest store.
*Fine-quality glass, china and
cutlery as well as an extensive
kitchen department.*

**John Lewis**
Visit www.johnlewis.com for
details of your nearest store.
*A one-stop shop for fine-
quality, good-value china,
glassware, cocktail equipment,
vases, bed linen and games.*

**The Laundry**
01594 841824
www.thelaundry.co.uk
*Beautiful 1930s- to 1950s-
inspired bed linen and
household textiles.*

**Paperchase**
Visit www.paperchase.co.uk
for details of your nearest store.
*Funky paper, pens and card,
plus invitations and placecards
in a choice of colours.*

**Emily Readett-Bayley**
www.emilyreadettbayley.co.uk
*Mother-of-pearl plates, bowls
and cutlery and bamboo
beakers and trays.*

**The White Company**
Visit
www.thewhitecompany.com
for your nearest store.
*Stylish bed linen, bedding,
towels and decorative
accessories. Also ironing water,
linen sprays and pillow mist.*

**Toast**
0844 55785200
www.toast.co.uk
*Beautiful items for the home.*

# US sources

**ABC Carpet & home**
www.abchome.com
*New and vintage linens,
silverware, crystal, tableware,
dinnerware, fabrics, and trim.
Great for gifts.*

**Are You Game?**
www.areyougame.com
*Carries all the most popular
games and puzzles as well as
many lesser-known options.*

**Bed, Bath, and Beyond**
www.bedbathandbeyond.com
*Linens, kitchenware, candles,
and glassware.*

**Chandler's Candle**
www.chandlerscandle.com
*Chic bamboo-look pillar
candles—also perfect gifts.*

**The Conran Shop**
407 East 59th Street
New York, NY 10022
(212) 755-9079
www.conran.com
*Stylish home furnishings,
vases, and kitchenware.*

**Crane & Co**
www.crane.com
*Fine stationery and invitations
for all occasions.*

**Crate & Barrel**
www.crateandbarrel.com
*Kitchenware, glassware,
cocktail equipment, china,
and linens.*

**Croquet.Com**
*Quality croquet sets for
every budget.*

**Fine Linens**
1193 Lexington Avenue
New York, NY 10028
(212) 737-2123
www.finelinens.com
*Linen placemats and
matching napkins.*

**Gamblers General Store**
www.gamblersgeneralstore.com
*Favorite casino games and
a huge choice of specialty
playing cards to purchase
online.*

**The Linen Closet Online**
www.thelinenclosetonline.com
*Fine French table linen
and placemats.*

**Paper Source**
www.paper-source.com
*Creative ideas for invitations
and thank-you cards.*

**Pier 1 Imports**
www.pier1.com
*Baskets, candles, table linen,
dinnerware, and glassware.*

**Portico Bed & Bath**
www.porticohome.com
*Fine linens and luxury beds.*

**Pottery Barn**
www.potterybarn.com
*Stylish, well-priced tabletop
essentials.*

**Yves Delorme**
www.yvesdelorme.com
*Luxurious linens.*

# Acknowledgments

Many thanks to Annabel Morgan and the editorial team at Ryland Peters & Small for tracking down and compiling many of the menus and recipes that appear in this book; and many thanks to Toni Kay for designing these beautiful pages.

I would also like to extend my gratitude to Tory Davis of Happy Kitchens, in Los Angeles, for advising on the Meals and Merriment chapter; Jeffrey Stamen, who eyeballed my wine pairings; and Louise Elliott for offering her conventional wisdom on several topics, from playing card games to shopping for groceries.

Finally, I am enormously grateful to my amazing, enthusiastic research assistant, Allison Bean, whose contributions pepper every chapter.